Keys to Parenting the Gifted Child

Third Edition

Sylvia B. Rimm, Ph.D.
Director, Family Achievement Clinic
Clinical Professor
Case Western Reserve University
School of Medicine
Cleveland, Ohio

Great Potential Press, Inc.
Scottsdale, Arizona

Copy Editor: Jen Ault
Cover design: MWVelgos Design
Interior design: The Printed Page

Published by Great Potential Press, Inc.
P.O. Box 5057
Scottsdale, AZ 85261

Printed on recycled paper

11 10 09 08 07   5 4 3 2 1

Library of Congress Cataloging-in-Publication Data

Rimm, Sylvia B.
  Keys to parenting the gifted child / Sylvia B. Rimm. — 3rd ed.
    p. cm.
  Includes index.
  ISBN 0-910707-74-X
  1. Gifted children—United States. 2. Parents of gifted children—United
States. 3. Gifted children—Education—United States. 4.
Parenting—United States. I. Title.
  HQ773.5.R55 2006
  649'.155—dc22
                                        2006022304

ISBN 13: 978-0-910707-74-9
ISBN 10: 0-910707-74-X

Dedication

To our children, Ilonna, David, Eric, and Sara,
and their spouses, Joseph, Janet, Allison, and Alan,
as they lovingly parent our grandchildren.

Contents

Introduction

Parenting our own four gifted children was our introduction to the unique joys and pressures of children who were in many ways both similar to and different from other children in their schools and neighborhoods. There were no books or courses to guide us along the way. Schools were doing little to understand or provide for our children's special learning needs, and parent advocacy had not yet begun in any organized fashion in the communities where we lived. Although gifted educational programs were available in some large cities and university centers, parents of gifted children in small cities, suburbs, or rural areas felt quite isolated when they recognized their children were learning at a different pace and depth than many of their peers.

As parents, we held feelings that were a mixture of awe, doubt, shame, and excitement. The awe and doubt were related to a fear that we as parents could not rely on memories of our families of origins for parenting strategies because we might not be intelligent enough to understand our gifted children's needs. Sometimes we felt that our children were, indeed, much smarter than we were. We were humbled by their high IQ scores, as are many parents of gifted children. Occasional feelings of shame stemmed from the fear that perhaps we had done something wrong by teaching our children before they were ready to learn, and sometimes we felt accused of this. Our excitement came from observations of our children's enthusiasm, curiosity, and intensity. They absolutely loved to learn.

Our children are grown now. Our parenting experiences led us to parenting advocacy and guided my own higher education toward the psychology of giftedness. In my Family Achievement Clinics, located in Wisconsin and Ohio, I have worked with many hundreds of gifted children, adolescents, and young adults. I have also worked with their parents and their teachers. This extensive experience has inspired me to share my opportunities with the many parents of gifted children through my books.

I hope that this book of keys helps you to feel less lonely as you parent your gifted children. It should also help you to feel more confident. You don't ever have to worry about parenting perfectly. This, like other perfectionisms, is not only impossible, it is not even normal or healthy. Your gifted children are likely to become learners, thinkers, workers, and contributors to our society if you love them, inspire them toward the joys of learning and thinking, and avoid some of the pitfalls that may mire other parents.

Our own children were taught that their giftedness carried with it a responsibility to make their own small contributions enthusiastically. Regardless of children's talents and intelligences, that is the most important message we need to give all children. In this way, each generation can move our world toward a more positive future.

I thank my children for being our first experiments and my husband for being such an effective partner in our parenting experiences. I acknowledge all the families and educators with whom I've worked in my clinics, as well as all the parents who have called in or sent in their parenting questions to me. Thank you also to my initial editor, Linda Turner, my current publisher, Jim Webb, and most important my assistants Joanne Riedl, Marilyn Knackert, Lori Butler, and Tammy Weisser for helping me communicate clearly and concisely these guidelines for parenting gifted children.

Part One

Your Gifted Child

1

So Your Child Is Gifted!

The first moment of holding your infant in your arms is engraved in your memory permanently. Just thinking about that wonderful moment brings a smile to your lips and joy to your heart. Your feeling of joy, however, was unrelated to your child's intelligence, creativity, or talent. It was related only to that wonderful bonding that comes with holding your newborn.

The wonderment of that initial bonding was mixed with some self-doubt, although by now the doubt may have temporarily disappeared. As mother or father, you may have felt concern about how capable you were of parenting this miraculous child and worried about whether you were truly ready for this new challenge. There were questions, perhaps openly discussed, perhaps quietly felt but untapped, of how your partner would experience parenting this infant with you. If you were a single parent, you felt the awesome responsibility of being the sole caretaker for your new baby. You definitely were not thinking of your child's talent. Your first wishes were just for good health and normalcy.

The first days and weeks of your child's life were filled with the basic activities of feeding, soothing, singing to, observing, and hugging this small bundle. As family and friends gathered around and commented on the baby's resemblances to you, your grandfather, or your mother-in-law, the observations about alertness or the kidding about musical or artistic talent began. These were not intended as communications about giftedness but were humorous comments only. Mainly, your wonderful baby was totally accepted. That was as it should have been and how it should always be.

The developmental needs and tasks of your children should always be at the forefront of your parenting. Your preschool gifted child, your school-age talented child, or your extremely intelligent teenager is always a baby, child, or adolescent first. Giftedness is only a secondary description. When this order is reversed, children suffer from pressures to be what they can't be—intellectual objects of their parents' creation instead of unique human beings.

I believe you know all of this already. You love your children so deeply, and you would not want to use them only as extensions of yourself. Nor would you want them to develop their capability to think without developing their ability to feel or love. Why, then, must you be reminded of what you already know? It is only because giftedness can be so reinforcing that it can lead even the most conscientious parent astray. Gifted children who learn quickly can become powerfully demanding, and the loving parents who see these children's hunger for stimulation can become enslaved in providing it. Here are some unusual examples:

> *Robbie, a high-energy baby, was rocked to sleep by the rhythms of mathematical facts. What began as a humorous game became an exciting challenge and a powerful manipulation. Robbie's hunger for mathematical learning hooked Mother into hours of repeated multiplication and division facts at bedtime. Crying was soothed by math, and although it was true that Robbie exhibited extreme mathematical talent by school age, he was also a peculiarly single-minded and powerful child. Although the rocking mathematics finally stopped, the search for appropriate mathematical stimulation for Robbie became a burning oppositional issue between parents and school. His unique math talent stole from him an emotionally healthy childhood.*

While still in her baby seat, Tanya peered at books as her daddy read to her. Her attention to color and words seemed unusual. Her love for being read to increased and expanded with a thirst that seemed to have no quenching. Mother and Father felt obligated to continuously read to Tanya. Her love of books was varied and extensive and far beyond a typical three-year-old's. Although wanting to enhance Tanya's interest, both parents became enslaved by a toddler whose hunger for books closed off other facets of her development. Tanya's parents actually believed they had no choice but to continue reading to Tanya as long as she demanded it.

Although rare, these two stories are real. The sometimes pressured but exciting environment that surrounds an extraordinary child who is very stimulated by learning can mislead even a loving, intelligent parent.

Gifted children exhibit talent early. They may speak in whole sentences when other similar-age children know only a few words. Some observe environmental details that aren't even noticed by others. Their questions may reveal a depth of understanding atypical of preschoolers. They may construct complex puzzles or toys or take toys apart in a manner that indicates extraordinary spatial understanding. Unusual sensitivity may be displayed. They may learn letters, numbers, colors, and shapes with speed and interest, come to adult-like mathematical conclusions, read spontaneously, have a sense of humor, or show extraordinary musical or artistic talent far beyond that of typical children. All these characteristics indicate giftedness.

Enjoy and encourage your children's love of learning, but foster their play, responsibility, imagination, affection, and fun so that they can grow as whole, as well as gifted, children.

2
Early Childhood Testing

You think your child is gifted, but you're not really sure. Research indicates that parents' perceptions of their preschool children's giftedness are usually accurate; however, you may not have confidence in your perceptions.

You've observed your friends' children: sometimes they seem as capable as your child, yet at other times those comparisons make your son or daughter seem unusually intelligent. Of course, you really prefer not making comparisons, but they happen anyway.

You've heard people say that *all* parents think their children are gifted, so you're wondering if your love, commitment, and joy in your children's accomplishments are magnifying your appraisal of their capabilities. Although you've read about child development and have observed other children of similar age, the feelings you have continue to be ambiguous. Since you don't want to omit appropriate stimulating environments from your children's initiation into school, you're considering whether your child should be tested by a psychologist.

Tests can supply you with important information about your child's intellectual giftedness, as long as you recognize that test results tend to be somewhat unreliable for preschool children. Scores can easily be lowered by shyness, a bad day, or merely fear of a particular tester. Lucky guesses can enhance the score a little, but slightly higher scores cause fewer problems than dramatically lowered scores.

Here are several very good reasons for having your preschool child tested:

1. Children who are intellectually gifted may benefit from early entrance to kindergarten, special curriculum planning within kindergarten, or a uniquely enriched preschool environment.

2. Test scores give quantitative data, which you may or may not choose to share with the school when communicating about your child's special needs. These quantitative data are usually based on norms that come from large samples, which permit you to compare your child's development to that of average children of similar age.

3. Weak areas may be discovered that otherwise might be masked by your child's intellectual giftedness. It is not unusual to find verbally gifted children who score poorly in tests of spatial abilities or small motor skills. Preschool testing permits you to assist your child in practicing these skills.

4. Test scores will give you confidence in your personal observations or correct them appropriately. For example, some children are very verbal but do not have abstract thinking skills yet and may appear to be gifted. Tests can prevent you from putting too much pressure on your child.

5. Early test scores provide baseline information that will help you to monitor your child's intellectual growth and progress.

Now that you've decided there may be a reason to test your child, you'll want to know where to find a tester.[1] If you're determining whether your child should be entered into school early or if you believe your child may require special programming, you could request that your local school psychologist do the testing. If gifted children are not considered to be within the domain of the school psychologist, you must find a private psychologist or university psychological center familiar with testing gifted children. There's reason to emphasize that the psychologist be familiar with the specialty of gifted children—not all psychologists are. Don't hesitate to ask. The director of gifted education in your state's department of education may be able to help you to find an appropriate tester, or you may check with your state association for gifted children. State associations are listed on the website of the National Association for Gifted Children (www.nagc.org).

There are individually-administered IQ tests that are appropriate for testing preschool gifted children. The *Wechsler Preschool and Primary Scale of Intelligence, Third Edition* (WPPSI-III) provides verbal, performance, and processing speed scores, and it is helpful to have all three. Its disadvantage is that scores do not go high enough to measure the abilities of profoundly gifted children. The same holds true for the *Stanford-Binet Intelligence Scale, Fifth Edition* (SB-V), but it, too, is a frequently used IQ test.

If your child is already reading and doing math calculations, an achievement test is also appropriate. The test should be given orally in a one-to-one setting to attain the most accurate results. Developmental delays in small muscle coordination or immaturity can lower the results of a written test for young children. A fair number of suitable tests are available that are relatively brief and provide reading and math information for a preschooler who may be demonstrating advanced skills that are more typical of school-age children. *The Peabody Individual Achievement Test, Revised* (PIAT-R) and *Woodcock-Johnson Achievement Test, Third Edition* (WJ-III) are commonly used by schools and clinics for measuring achievement individually.

Age four is usually early enough for a first testing if you require the information for school decision-making. Because gifted children learn so rapidly, there may be a need for further achievement testing just before school entrance for academic placement. Generally, there is no further need for IQ testing for three or four years unless test results don't seem to match teacher or parent observations.

Prekindergarten screenings conducted by schools are not intended to assess giftedness. Although they do provide the school with some important developmental information, they cannot be used to measure the extent of children's intellectual giftedness or academic achievement because the difficulty of the test items is not likely to be sufficient.

If you sense that your child is gifted but there are no early entrance decisions or specific curriculum changes that need to be considered, it's probably better to postpone testing until first grade when scores become more reliable. Many gifted children learn to read only at the typical age in first grade, and for those children, individual psychoeducational testing can wait until school age.

3

Selecting a Preschool

In many ways, the guidelines for selecting a school for your gifted preschooler are identical to those for any child. There are only a few special considerations, and these are shared as final criteria to consider.

You may be looking for daycare so that you can continue your careers, or you may only be looking for part-time opportunities for your children. The criteria are surprisingly similar except that consistency and communication between home and school are even more critical if your children spend more of their day away from home. Communication between school and home is important, not only because you will feel more secure about the environment being provided for your children, but also because you, as parents, can share in your children's developmental milestones, even though you are not available to witness them at all times. Exchanging a daily journal can facilitate that communication. Your childcare providers can be asked to document your children's daily accomplishments, and they are more likely to understand how important this is for you. Here are other criteria for you to consider:

> ➤ Warm positive atmosphere. Your visit to the preschool setting should provide you with a sense that the childcare providers are loving toward all the children. If staff members seem to be targeting children who are troublemakers

in their conversations with others, consider that your child could become one of those children, and that would not be a good school start. If instead they emphasize optimistic approaches to problem solving, this implies that their approach is healthier.

➤ Stability of staff. Stability of staff helps the consistency of programming. Schools that have a history of continuous staff turnover may not be selecting staff well or not training them sufficiently. It is also possible that the leadership of the school is inadequate. Obviously, occasional changes in staff are normal. You can best obtain that information from other parents who have had children at the school for a while. If teachers have left with frequency, you may also want to ask about the reason.

➤ Classroom organization and control. A too-orderly preschool can be stifling to children, but reasonable organization and limit-setting are critical to a child's early learning of responsibility and self-discipline. Routines that teach children good manners, clean-up responsibilities, consideration for others, and respect for teachers will provide good preparation for school and life. Disorganized, out-of-control class environments may cause feelings of insecurity for preschool children. Gifted children may be especially sensitive to the disorder.

➤ Opportunities for creative expression and curiosity. Toys and equipment should include painting and drawing supplies, small and large building blocks, pretend and imaginative toys, as well as sturdy outdoor equipment. Opportunities go beyond equipment. An atmosphere where children are expected to explore, create and invent, feel and touch, rather than simply copy adult direction and fill in lines or work pages, underscores a creative environment. Observe the classroom to determine if children are encouraged to question. Observe teachers' responses to children who ask many questions. Gifted children will be turned off if they aren't encouraged to follow their interests. If structure is too rigid, children will learn to follow, but their curiosity is stifled.

➤ Fostering the love of books. Almost every good daycare center or preschool encourages the love of literature, reading, and drama, and this is particularly important because the love of books is a prerequisite to the love of learning. Several story hours a day are desirable and should not be replaced by a convenient television set; the television should either be a very small part of children's learning in preschool or not be present at all. Babies recognize familiar words as early as eight months, which suggests reading to children can begin before their first birthday.

➤ Music, dance, and movement. Creative movement provides opportunities for the development of children's love of music and rhythm. Dance or some form of moving to music should be part of almost every preschool day. Skipping, hopping, jumping, and marching to music are appropriate examples. Many schools elaborate far beyond these basics.

➤ Outdoor play and explorations. The exploration of nature may be limited at urban centers, but learning about weather, animals, and nature can be carried out at parks and playgrounds and is as important to gifted children as learning from books. Observation skills and curiosity are encouraged by an awareness of the outdoors, as are sensitivity to animal families and relationships between people and nature.

➤ Value systems. The preschool's religious points of view and values about honesty, respect, animal life, conservation, and so on should be a reasonable match with your family values. Although they need not be identical, they should at least complement what you believe is appropriate for your children.

➤ Freedom to choose within limitations. Some school curriculums are the same for the entire class; others permit children to make all of the choices for activities. Neither extreme is productive for gifted children in the long run. Rigid preschool lessons will not allow for individual giftedness if all children are working on similar skills; therefore, rigid lessons will not provide challenges for your gifted child. Allowing the children to make all of the choices is also risky. Gifted children are likely to select and pursue areas that interest them, but they may ignore or neglect some of the more boring skills they may require for kindergarten. Furthermore, a school that permits children to make all the choices empowers preschoolers too much. The children may assume school will always be that way and balk at later school environments that feel restrictive by comparison.

➤ Academic preparation. Preschools should provide some academic preparation for kindergarten. Gifted children often express a thirst for academic learning that tempts parents and teachers to provide more and more. Some gifted four-year-olds may wish to read or do math all day, and for those that show readiness, a little time each day is appropriate and important. A more holistic approach is as important for gifted children as it is for all children. It is not appropriate for any child's self-esteem to be based only on that child's capacity to learn.

➤ Recognition of giftedness. The staff of an excellent preschool shouldn't feel threatened by parents' discussion of their child's advanced abilities. If a teacher rapidly changes the subject or responds that all the children in the school are gifted, that teacher is not likely to be responsive to your gifted child's individual needs. A response that recognizes individual differences and also refers to some other children's special needs can reassure you that you are in an environment that values your child's unique creative and learning abilities in a balanced way.

First-hand observations of a preschool class in session, using a checklist, and taking notes will help you to evaluate these criteria. An interview with the teacher and some telephone calls to other parents will assist you in gathering other information.

If you are having difficulties in choosing between schools, rate each criterion on a one to five scale and add up your final score. Don't let the numbers make your final decision for you, but permit them to influence your decision-making in a more concrete way. You may feel disappointed when you find that few preschools satisfy all your criteria. This is only the beginning of realism as it relates to future school selections. Schools can hardly ever afford to be perfect, so you'll need to have realistic standards. Many fine schools are available.

4

When to Start Kindergarten

Dates for kindergarten entrance are established based on the developmental readiness typical for most five-year-olds. It is logical to have a specific date, and it is just as logical that there should be a basis for exceptions. Some states allow exceptions based on testing; other states permit no departures from the deadline date. Even within states, school districts may have a variety of entrance dates, rules, and variations.

In some places, it is considered fashionable to delay children's entrance to kindergarten, especially for boys, in the belief that an extra year of maturity will make it more likely that these children will become "best" students and leaders in their classes. Teachers often remind parents that this extra year also improves their competitive sports performance and their confidence. Although there do not appear to be data that suggest improved sports performances or confidence, there are data on achievement, and the research has not born out what appeared to many parents and teachers to be intuitively true and common sense. Findings indicate that children who are held back from entering kindergarten do *not* do as well academically on the average as children who are entered in a timely manner. Furthermore, long-term studies have shown decreases in IQ scores related to being held back, as well as more behavioral problems among boys in middle and high school.

Research findings are based on populations, and although they are helpful guides in decision-making, you'll want a professional individual assessment before you make a final decision. School or private psychologists who specialize in working with gifted children can evaluate your child's school readiness.

If your child's tests are in the very superior IQ range, your child may be better off being young in the class. Research in the field of gifted education continuously finds that children who are accelerated or entered early achieve better with the additional challenge. Socially, they adjust as well as gifted children of typical kindergarten entrance age who have not been entered early or accelerated.[2]

Girls tend to mature earlier than boys. Although children are sometimes actually less mature than their classmates, at other times, symptoms of immaturity indicate that a child has not been given enough independence. These same symptoms could also mean a child has been given too much power and has not learned to respect adult leadership. Thus, symptoms of immaturity may merely represent inappropriate behaviors that can be changed. Some teachers may assume that shy children are immature, when their shyness is actually related to their temperament or to their lack of group experience. Entering school in a timely way will increase social experience and may actually facilitate maturity. If your child has a shy temperament, he or she may nevertheless be very capable and shouldn't be penalized for having a quiet personality. By preventing a shy child from experiencing kindergarten in a timely manner, you may actually be hurting confidence by encouraging the child's hesitancy. There is almost no good reason to prevent intellectually gifted children from entering school at the usual age unless they have verified learning disabilities.

If the school offers optional early entrance, intellectual and academic assessments provide your best objective guides, along with using instruments like the *Iowa Acceleration Scale*.[3] If your children are tall, it may help you to feel more comfortable about early entrance, even though there is no research indicating that height makes a difference in either intellectual or social adjustment. If sports that require height are your first priority, that may cause you some hesitancy about early entrance. However, if you base your decision on sports capability, it will indicate to your children that your first school priority is not academic, so don't be surprised if your children value sports more than learning.

A decision for your child has to be made individually and carefully. Such subjective factors as differing opinions between the child's parents, the classroom makeup of a particular school, and the age of siblings are additional subtleties that influence your decision-making. Although all these issues require some consideration, the dominant reason that is frequently heard, but is inappropriate, is the parent's wish that the child be at the top of the class academically. Actually, this is a very competitive wish that could doom your child to underachievement. Because the child is unlikely to be challenged for the first few years and will excel easily, when challenge does come along, your child is likely to be unaccustomed to study and perseverance. The fear of disappointing parents and self at not being at the top inhibits the child from taking the risk of working hard. It's easier for the child to blame teachers or boredom than to question the pressure he or she feels at no longer being smartest in the class.

If your child is younger in the class, there can actually be some benefit if your child is not working as hard as expected. You can explain that he or she will have to work a little harder to keep up with children who are a little older. If your child is oldest by far and intellectually gifted as well, parents may find it a bit harder to find encouraging words when school grades drop.

Intellectually gifted children, like all children who enter kindergarten, should have opportunities for learning new academic material. For some gifted children, this requires early entrance to kindergarten. For many, the typical entrance age will be suitable.

5

Enhancing Learning in the Family

Parents can experience the joy of enhancing their children's learning in many shared ways, beginning with encouraging a love of reading and including an appreciation of culture, the arts, the environment, exploration, science, government, and the world community. The list goes on, and information in this key includes only a few suggestions. Additional Reading at the end of this book lists numerous books to help you to expand your children's learning. Libraries and bookstores can provide many more.

Your home provides the first learning laboratory. Kitchen science and cooking are effective teaching tools. Encyclopedias, atlases, and globes help to expand your children's horizons and their love of geography beyond the living room. Play dough, water colors, sand boxes, and clay permit the creative exploration of the arts. Puzzles, Legos®, blocks, and other kinds of building toys teach spatial skills and encourage creativity. Board games help children to learn both winning and losing, and are important for teaching a healthy, competitive spirit. A piano or guitar being played by an amateur musician–parent becomes the basis for many sing-alongs and play-alongs. Stores are filled with records and tapes, and listening to taped stories (without pictures) encourages children's listening and imagination skills. Dancing to recorded music facilitates your children's coordination and their love of music. When parents join in the dance, families become less inhibited. Add ballet slippers to your dance performances, and even the awkward feel graceful.

Be sure to explore your community resources. Art museums, parks, conservatories, museums of natural history, aquariums, observatories, nature centers, children's museums, theaters, and concert halls may be closer and less expensive than you realize.

Trips or visits outside your community increase in value if your children are involved in the planning. Learning how to send for brochures, maps, and travel information is a good skill for children to develop. Trips become more interesting for them if they can participate in planning the routes and places to visit.

Cameras and tape recorders increase the depths of learning when children travel and preserve the memories and knowledge they obtain. A microcasette tape recorder can serve as an oral journal for children, as well as an interviewing tool for friends they meet along the way. Interviewing a forest ranger on video or tape recorder may forever preserve messages about conservation, and your children will remember them better through the personalization, involvement, and repetition.

When you can tie travel or community activities to your children's school learning, this adds relevance to what school contributes. Farms are wonderful exploration areas for urban and suburban children. Seeing sugar cane being grown in Louisiana or corn in Iowa makes these products much more meaningful when they are studied in school. Talking to growers or farmers about their problems and recording the conversations provides special insights for your children and their classmates. Cities are also important to visit and learn about; every city has a unique history. Remember that talking with different people adds depth to every visit.

History comes alive with a visit to a great grandparent's home or to a home for senior citizens. Social histories based on questions planned together are exciting for your children, for you, and for the elderly.

Of course, there is some risk of overwhelming your children with too much culture. If you're enthusiastic and they're uninterested, it may be a signal for you either to slow down or to do some adult activities without them.

If there are two parents in the family, it's important to preserve positive, united interest. Unfortunately, if one parent voices dislike for the ballet or art, some children are likely to resist exploring those cultural experiences. The key seems to be to develop genuine interests and enthusiasm and to avoid overdoing.

Although schools invest the most time into teaching your children skills, parents truly are very important teachers. If you can avoid putting pressure on your children and recognize that overload can cause disinterest, your modeling of a love of life and learning will provide the very best of opportunities for your children.

6

Learning to Love Reading

Gifted children often anticipate with excitement the opportunity to learn to read, and they enthusiastically share their first conquests of the written word with their parents and teachers. Some gifted children learn to read as early as age two, while others don't read until they're taught in first grade. Enthusiasm about the preschool child's early reading can be positive and encouraging, but parents should be careful not to exhibit their children by bragging about their early reading or urging them to read aloud to all visitors. There's the risk that their children will only read for attention instead of for the intrinsic love of books and stories.

For students who love reading, school is very likely to be a positive experience. However, some gifted children struggle with learning to read, and the educational process becomes more difficult. Because good reading skill is often equated with intelligence, these children may lose confidence quickly. Here are suggestions to generally encourage the love of reading for all children, along with special recommendations for gifted children who have reading problems. It is important to guide your children who cope with reading problems toward self-confidence and independence, despite their reading struggles.

> ➤ Family reading should begin with infants and extend throughout life. There are no grade or age limits at which family reading should stop. Reading together, either aloud

or silently, creates an atmosphere for children to love books.

➤ As a family, read biographies of people who have made contributions. Gifted children have often been inspired to achieve by role models in biographies.

➤ Permit children to stay up half an hour later at night if they're in their beds reading to themselves (children don't usually like to sleep; it's adults who do).

➤ Encourage children to read whatever they like during that time before going to sleep. Don't insist they read grade-level material. Comics, cartoons, sports magazines, easy material, and books read multiple times are all good for reading enjoyment. If they love reading, they will expand their interests as their reading improves.

➤ Model reading by keeping books, newspapers, and magazines around that your children see you enjoy.

➤ Become a regular visitor with your children to public libraries. Encourage them to attend story hours at an early age, and when they're old enough to ride to the library on their bikes or on a bus, encourage their regular visits. Wander through public libraries in new cities as part of your travel plan and encouragement of curiosity.

➤ When shopping in malls or on main streets, stop by bookstores and browse or perhaps purchase books. Encourage your children to choose books they'll read and later cherish.

➤ Monitor and limit TV watching and video games. If this becomes a power struggle, you may find using a plug lock[4] very effective. Too much TV takes time away from reading.

➤ Include computers and the Internet in your children's opportunities for reading. Electronic books will be common in the future.

Intellectually gifted children are usually excellent readers, but some are not strong readers and may even have reading disabilities. Disabilities can produce anxieties for all children, but for gifted children, the disparity between their thinking ability and their reading capabilities can cause considerable frustration or embarrassment. Here are some suggestions should you observe a reading problem:

➤ Ask your school psychologist or private clinic to evaluate your child for a reading disability.

➤ If that yields no explanation, you may want to have your child evaluated for a specific reading disability called Scotopic Sensitivity Syndrome.[5] It is a biological disorder which is typically inherited. Thus, a parent or an aunt or uncle is likely to have a history of an early reading problem. Scotopic Sensitivity Syndrome is helped dramatically by colored lenses. Different colors seem to work for different people.

➤ Don't force poor readers to read aloud.

➤ Don't force your children to read aloud under unpredictable or embarrassing circumstances or at home if you think you may unintentionally convey anxieties about your children's reading to them. Most parents feel tense when poor readers read aloud to them. As adult readers, children who were forced to read aloud will rarely find oral reading important. Children should read aloud if they choose to do so.

➤ Encourage children to read to their younger siblings, provided these siblings aren't better readers than they are. They shouldn't do this in your presence, but alone with their sisters or brothers.

➤ Ask your children's teachers to permit them to read aloud to preschool or kindergarten children. The books are easy, and the simplicity of the reading and the enthusiastic

receiving audience of small children will build poor readers' confidence and their love of reading.

➤ Encourage children to read stories while listening to CDs
of the stories. Don't hover over them to be sure they're
actually reading; eventually they will.

➤ Don't read homework instructions to your children.
Instead, encourage them to read the instructions to themselves several times. Also, suggest that they may "whisper
read" them (reading in a whispered voice to oneself). This
helps them to concentrate and understand the instructions
better. This seems to yield a great improvement in some
children's comprehension.

➤ If your children continue to require assistance in understanding assignments because of reading problems, tape
record the instructions and let them listen while they're
reading them. It is better to listen to the tape recorder than
to become dependent on parent or teacher attention. They
can stop the tape recorder, reverse it, and listen as many
times as it takes for them to understand.

➤ Content area textbooks such as social studies or science
should be made available to children on CDs for simulta-
neous listening while reading. This will usually increase
their reading vocabulary, as well as prevent feelings of inadequacy that arise from their lack of content knowledge.

➤ Don't assume poor readers are less intelligent because they
don't read well.

➤ Don't unintentionally label poor readers negatively at home
or school through referential comments—that is, by talking
about their problems to other adults within their hearing.

➤ Don't take responsibility for poor readers because they
can't read; help them to become independent. Identify
ways by which they can carry on activities independently

by using audio equipment or illustrations rather than people. Continued one-to-one help will only encourage dependency and make them feel less intelligent.

➤ Encourage poor readers to become actively involved in drama and forensics. They may require a cassette recorder to help them prepare their presentations, but mastery of verbal material will help build their confidence.

➤ Be patient and supportive. If your children continue to read in an unpressured way, they may eventually master and learn to love reading. Many gifted adults have a history of early reading problems.

7

School Identification of Giftedness

Your gifted children may have been identified for school programs to enhance and encourage their talents, or you may be confused because, indeed, one or more of your children have not been identified despite your belief that they need special programming.

The first federal definition of giftedness used by schools as a basis for identification was included in a national report by Marland in 1972. It is important because it was the basis for legislation in many states and is still used in many school districts. That definition follows:

> *Gifted and talented children are those identified by professionally qualified persons who, by virtue of outstanding abilities, are capable of high performance. These are children who require differentiated educational programs and services beyond those normally provided by the regular school program in order to realize their contribution to self and society.*
>
> *Children capable of high performance include those with demonstrated achievement and/or potential in any of the following areas:*
>
> *1. General intellectual ability*
> *2. Specific academic aptitude*

3. Creative or productive thinking
4. Leadership ability
5. Visual and performing arts
6. Psychomotor ability

Public Law 100-297 (1988) provided schools with the most current national definition of giftedness. A similar definition was recommended in the 1993 federal report, *National Excellence: A Case for Developing America's Talent* (Public Law 100-297, Sec. 4103. Definitions):

> *The term "gifted and talented students" means children and youth who give evidence of high performance capability in areas such as intellectual, creative, artistic, or leadership capacity, or in specific academic fields, and who require services or activities not ordinarily provided by the school in order to fully develop such capabilities.*

Another definition popularly used by schools was developed by Joseph Renzulli at the University of Connecticut. He based his definition upon descriptions of creatively productive persons who made important contributions to society. His definition of gifted behavior reflects an interaction among three basic clusters of human traits—above average general and/or specific ability, high levels of task commitment, and creativity. Children who possess, or are capable of developing, this composite set of traits and applying them to any potentially valuable area of human performance are defined by him as gifted.

Even if your children are gifted, your children's school may not be providing for their types of giftedness. Schools and states differ in their approaches to identifying children for gifted programming, and many do not even provide special programs. Furthermore, some schools may have programs that only provide for certain kinds of giftedness; for example, they may only provide for high achievers and neglect those children who possess leadership, creative, and artistic abilities. Intellectual giftedness is the most frequent type of giftedness that schools provide for, and even that may not be adequately provided for within your school district. In addition, gifted underachievers and learning-disabled, gifted students are not included in programs in many school districts, despite their special needs.

The percentages of students included in gifted programming vary significantly. The Marland definition of giftedness suggested a minimum of 3 to 5% of a school's population. Some school districts identify an arbitrary 5%. Other districts boast of broader programs that may include as many as 25% of their students in some kinds of gifted programming. A recent report indicated that four states identified more than 10% of their student enrollment as gifted and talented, while 21 states identified fewer than 5%.

For many years, economically disadvantaged students and minority groups were greatly underserved, particularly when IQ score cutoffs were the main identification technique. More recently, efforts to appropriately identify and program for these populations have increased dramatically. Despite the improvement in identification, Native-American, African-American, and Hispanic populations are still often underidentified and underserved.

Some school districts use only group IQ scores for identification of their students. Other schools may include creativity tests, student products (such as artwork or music), peer or parent nominations, and/or teacher recommendations. The identification process may seem quite confusing to parents, and this key cannot be effective in clarifying every school's rationale for their identification methods of gifted children. However, parents shouldn't hesitate to ask questions of school personnel. Schools will undoubtedly be happy to communicate their philosophies and selection criteria.

IQ measures continue to be priority tests for use in identifying children's giftedness. The initials IQ stand for "intelligence quotient." The term came from tests that were initially created by Alfred Binet in France in 1905; he used a chronological/mental age formula to predict whether children were sufficiently intelligent to benefit from schooling. IQ tests have been changed and revised many times since Binet's first tests, and educators have become much more sophisticated in their use. Although these tests are often still referred to as intelligence tests, they only measure some kinds of intelligence, and scores are affected by cultural environments and learning opportunities.

Despite the problems of IQ tests, they can still be used cautiously to predict how well children will do in various educational environments. IQ scores from group intelligence tests are typically used to identify gifted students because they are less costly than individual tests. Some of the better-known group intelligence tests are the *Cognitive Abilities Test,* the *Henmon-Nelson Test of Mental Ability,* the *SRA Primary Mental Abilities Tests,* and the *Otis-Lennon Mental Ability Test.* Despite their comparatively low cost and convenient group administration, they have shortcomings. Group tests tend to be less reliable and less valid than individual tests. Also, children who are not motivated produce lower IQ scores than their apparent abilities indicate. Group tests are mainly verbal and dependent upon actual school achievement; therefore, they are biased against nonverbal gifted children or children who come from disadvantaged environments. Group tests tend to be unreliable at high IQ levels; a few chance errors may substantially lower a gifted student's IQ score. They are typically timed, and children who write or think slowly may be penalized. Despite the problems with group tests, children who score high on them are always capable and certainly should be included in gifted programs. However, other identification methods should be used for identifying unmotivated or culturally deprived students.

Some schools also administer individual IQ tests to gifted students. These must be administered by the school psychologist, and each administration takes approximately two hours. Because of the expense involved, most schools do not test entire populations but only students who pass a preliminary group screening or those who have special problems. These tests will be discussed in Key 8.

Schools usually identify specific academic talent by using standardized achievement tests, such as the *Iowa Tests of Basic Skills,* the *Metropolitan Achievement Tests,* the *SRA Achievement Series,* the

California Achievement Tests, or the *California Test of Basic Skills.* Two important problems with standardized achievement test scores should be highlighted. The first concerns the grade-equivalent score. Grade equivalent refers to the average score earned by children at a particular grade level on a particular test, not to the grade level at which a specific gifted child can function well in the classroom. Sometimes parents assume that if gifted fourth graders perform well at the eighth-grade equivalent on math achievement tests, they can perform successfully at the eighth-grade level. Although the children may be good math students, they probably lack many skills of average eighth graders and many more compared to gifted eighth graders. Grade-equivalent scores can be misleading and should only be used as indicators that students need special challenge. Further diagnostic testing should be used to determine the specific skills.

The second problem of standardized achievement test scores is the low ceiling score of typical achievement tests. Most achievement tests are not sufficiently difficult to measure the high abilities, knowledge, and skill levels of very able children. Many students may score at the ceiling level or "top out" of the test. Thus, it is sometimes assumed that all of these children are equally talented and need a similar skill development program. In fact, after diagnostic testing, or even with the use of more difficult achievement tests, a wide range of advanced skill levels is found among these children.

Creativity tests can be used to confirm a teacher's observations about the creativeness of one or more students or to identify creative students whose talents are not obvious in the classroom. Creativity tests are far from perfect. Scores from a single creativity test might be quite misleading. A student who in fact does extraordinarily creative work in art or science can produce an average creativity score. Creativity is a complex ability that can take many forms. IQ tests do not measure creativity. Data from creativity tests should be combined with observations to make decisions regarding creativity. Most schools that attempt to identify creativity use at least two forms of identification.

There are two main categories of creativity tests: divergent thinking measures, and inventories that assess personality and biographical traits. Divergent thinking tests require students to think of many answers to open-ended problems, such as giving unusual uses for a newspaper or a brick or imagining consequences of unlikely events. Divergent thinking tests are scored using criteria such as fluency (the number of ideas produced) and originality (uniqueness of the ideas). The *Torrance Tests of Creative Thinking* are the most widely used divergent thinking tests.

PRIDE, GIFT, GIFFI I, and *GIFFI II* instruments are inventories used to assess personality and biographical information. Such personality traits as curiosity, humor, and risk-taking appear repeatedly in studies of creative, productive people.

Teachers also use checklists in the identification of creativity, and sometimes to identify leadership characteristics. Parent and peer questionnaires are sometimes used for the identification of all kinds of giftedness, but particularly the areas of creativity and leadership.

Identification of children who are gifted in visual and performing arts, if indeed schools provide such programs, are usually quite specific to the particular art form. Creativity tests have not been found to be effective for specific arts identification. Thus, artistic products, such as portfolios, are typically used for identification of the visual arts, and actual tryout performances are used for music or drama.

Very few general elementary or secondary public schools sponsor programs for students talented in the visual and performing arts. Art and music teachers try to cultivate their students' special talents, but more frequently, students are advised to take private lessons outside school. Unfortunately for economically disadvantaged students who may be talented in the visual and performing arts, outside teachers may simply not be a practical economical alternative. However, many large cities and some states do provide magnet specialty schools in these areas.

8

Individual Evaluations

Many parents are confused about whether to have their gifted children evaluated privately and, if so, when the testing should be done. Testing and evaluation of preschool children were discussed in Key 2. This key relates to specific evaluation concerns for school-age children.

Whether or not your children have been identified by the gifted identification system of your children's school, you may wish to have further individual evaluations conducted either by the school or by a private psychologist. If you want information for acceleration or enrichment considerations or if you believe your children are underachieving, further evaluation is appropriate. If you suspect your children's school is not providing appropriately for your gifted children, individual testing can provide support for your assumptions or may verify that your children's needs are being met in the school program. Career preference testing may also be important for your teenage gifted children if they are multitalented and are confused about how they can direct their multiple talents toward future careers. Parents can request testing by the school psychologist even if such evaluation is not part of the school's usual identification procedures.

When schools do not include testing of gifted students as a psychological responsibility, you may need to search out private psychologists, even though only a very small percentage of psychologists have backgrounds in the area of giftedness. University centers that have programs for gifted educators are likely to have facilities for psychological assessment of gifted children.

School or private psychologists are likely to use one of several intelligence tests. The most frequently used series are the *Wechsler Intelligence Scales,* including preschool, school-age, and adolescent/adult versions. These tests are listed in Commonly Used Tests at the end of this book. The *Wechsler Intelligence Scale for Children, Fourth Edition* (WISC-IV) provides Verbal Comprehension, Perceptual Reasoning, Working Memory, and Processing Speed IQ scores, along with the Full-Scale IQ score. It's possible for children to be gifted in some areas and only average or above average in other areas. Although the Wechsler tests are helpful for identifying strengths and weaknesses, it is possible to score only as high as 155 on these tests using the traditionally normed tests, and this score can be achieved only if children are gifted in all areas.

The preschool WPPSI-III and the school-age WISC-IV provide tables of age-equivalent scores. When these are used in conjunction with the chronological/mental age formula recommended by Alfred Binet in his original test, there is almost no ceiling for young elementary children. By the teenage years, however, even the age-equivalent scores have significant limitations for identifying profoundly gifted students.

As in the case with testing young children mentioned in Key 2, the *Stanford-Binet, Fifth Edition* may be preferred by some psychologists. However, this test also has serious ceiling limitations for testing profoundly gifted children.

Individual achievement tests, including the *Peabody Individual Achievement Test,* the *Woodcock-Johnson Achievement Test,* and the *Wide Range Achievement Test*, are typically administered by psychologists. School districts may choose from a wide range of other achievement tests.

The SAT and ACT tests, which are widely used for college admission, are often used for middle school children to provide opportunities for these children to demonstrate knowledge and reasoning skill beyond what is typical for chronological age peers. The talent search program use of these tests is discussed in Key 15.

If parents are concerned about their children's symptoms of stress, rebelliousness, or depression, they may request that a psychologist administer personality assessments or projective tests. The results from those assessments can help in understanding pressures, power issues, or frustrations gifted children may feel.

Psychologists are trained to interpret for parents all cognitive and affective testing, and therefore you should not hesitate to ask questions until you feel comfortable about understanding how to guide your children toward appropriate educational and vocational choices. Individual testing can be very important for making educational plans for your children. Acceleration and grade-skipping decisions should not be made without the guidance of such detailed evaluations. Because evaluations for gifted children are typically related to mental health issues, rather than learning needs alone, mental health insurance sometimes provides partial payment for private evaluations.

Many career tests can be used for guiding gifted children toward higher education and decision-making for their futures, but the specific test is less critical than the counselor. It is important that the career counselor have an in-depth understanding of the many advanced careers available to very talented young adults. The issues of multiple talents and interests should be combined with the counselor's knowledge of actual opportunities for positions in a field. It is unwise to assume that gifted children should follow only their immediate interests if that career direction does not provide opportunity for complexity and growth. There is also the risk that gifted young people may invest eight to 10 years in preparation for an interesting career in which they will not be able to find employment. In addition to being guided by a knowledgeable counselor, students should take the initiative to interview people who are employed in the careers they may be considering.

If evaluations are interpreted by persons familiar with the special issues related to giftedness, you may be able to prevent some of the pitfalls and pressures that can affect your children because of their giftedness. Furthermore, the specialists who conduct the evaluation may be able to assist you in advocating for your gifted children's educational and psychological needs.

9

Subject Acceleration and Individualized Instruction

If you become aware of an actual lack of academic challenge for your gifted child, you will want to explore ways to obtain a more stimulating and challenging curriculum. This lack of challenge may be brought to your attention by your child or your child's teacher. Gifted resource programs, classroom enrichment, and subject acceleration provide appropriate curriculum adjustments for most gifted children.

Although grade skipping is usually the preferred arrangement for students who have very high IQs and strong overall achievement, many gifted children excel in only one or two academic areas. These children are not good candidates for entire grade skips; however, they seem to thrive when a particular subject area is either compacted or skipped entirely.

Rapid progression through a subject by acceleration can involve having children do all the basic work in a subject without doing as many examples or practice skills, thus accomplishing it in much less time. Skipping is preferred if tests indicate the child already shows competence in the subject and can, therefore, go on to the next grade level in that particular subject. Acceleration in one or two subjects can be accomplished within the classroom, or students could actually move to the next grade for a subject skip.

Surprisingly, unlike grade skipping, subject skipping has not been well researched. Nevertheless, it is not only frequently used by schools, but also is often recommended by teachers. In contrast to the negative attitudes often exhibited toward grade skipping, many educators feel very comfortable about subject acceleration. Sometimes subject skipping is the only acceleration needed for students who have a specific academic talent. Subject skipping can also be used experimentally as a prior step to grade skipping if parents and teachers are uncertain about how the student will adjust to a grade skip.

Making a decision for subject acceleration is much simpler than for grade skipping. Although IQ tests may be used, they may not even be required. Individual achievement tests in reading, mathematics, science, spelling, or social studies; end-of-book tests; or class performance serve satisfactorily to indicate to educators and parents that students are already competent in most of the topics to be taught during the school year ahead. If the student demonstrates approximately 70% competency, it is certainly not logical to devote a year to teaching what this student could probably learn individually in a few days or weeks. Although it is important that missed skills be learned, a year devoted to this same curriculum would be counterproductive. Not only is the class likely to be boring to the student, it gives the student the message that there is little to learn in school.

After the student demonstrates competency, the decision of how to challenge the student within a subject will depend on such variables as school scheduling, teacher flexibility, other students in the class, the subject itself, and the child's age and temperament.

School scheduling that provides the same time block for a subject in two adjacent grades may allow a child to simply go into the next grade classroom for a subject. For example, the simplest curriculum adjustment for a first grader who has demonstrated math competence could be one in which the student goes to the second-grade classroom down the hall at 10:15 each day for math.

Concurrent subject scheduling is more likely to occur in primary rather than higher grades.

Sometimes attempts to have a child go to the next grade result in so much disruption of the child's schedule that it seems wiser to adjust curriculum within the classroom. This alternative will require teacher flexibility. The teacher is already working with students who have a range of skills and abilities within the classroom, and some teachers may not be willing to add yet another level beyond the grade he or she is teaching at present.

If there are other students in the class at a similar skill level, this facilitates either out-of-class or in-class acceleration. It is always easier for teachers to make exceptions in the curriculum when many students are involved. In addition, most students enjoy being part of a small group and feel less isolated than if they are the only one sent to another class or doing special work.

The nature of the subject to be accelerated must also be considered in the curriculum adjustment. Such subjects as mathematics and spelling lend themselves to individualized curriculum, but much of reading, social studies, and science is enhanced by group discussion or interaction. Components of each of the latter subjects can also be individualized, but students may truly lose some important perspectives if they study these subjects in isolation.

Last and most important is consideration of the age and temperament of the individual child. Younger children may feel more hesitant about leaving their classroom and joining another class. Shy children may find it more difficult than more socially comfortable children. Although none of these variables should preclude encouraging a child to risk the new experience, parents and teachers should be sensitive to signs of tension that indicate that the child is feeling stress. Initial tensions should be expected, however, and modifications should not be discontinued immediately. On the other hand, if the child continues to show signs of stress when joining another class or working alone, other alternatives should be explored.

Although some gifted children thrive with individualized instruction, others feel isolated and prefer class participation. It's important to recognize that children who work independently and seem content with individual curriculum nevertheless need feedback and interest from teachers. Sometimes teachers assume that gifted children require almost no teaching and interaction. Even though these assumptions are correct for a very limited number of students, most gifted students require the same encouragement and interest on which other students thrive. They simply need it at an accelerated pace and at a more in-depth level.

If a gifted child does not achieve in an individualized curriculum, it is important to realize that this is not an indicator that the child does not require challenge, only a symptom that the child requires an adjustment in teaching style.

10

Grade Skipping

For a small percentage of gifted children, skipping one or more grades may be the best approach for providing academic challenge. Parents and teachers often are reluctant to recommend grade skipping from concern that it places too much pressure on the children and that the skipping will negatively affect their social adjustment. Adults may want to remind themselves, however, that doing nothing is also making a decision. If they don't make accommodations to challenge their gifted children or students, this gives these children a message that academic challenge is a lesser priority than social conformity and that hard work is unimportant. This message of conformity may cause problems when children become adolescents. Teenagers may repeat the message in another form and tell their parents and teachers that social life is their main priority and that they don't want to work hard on their schoolwork.

Individual tests of academic ability (IQ) and achievement, discussed in Key 8, are the most important evaluative measures used for acceleration decision-making. Despite the many documented problems of IQ tests, they provide good predictors for successful grade skipping.

The availability and quality of school enrichment programs and the academic makeup of the child's present class, as well as that of the class to which the child would be advanced, should also be considered. Peer academic environments can vary from grade to grade, and sometimes a challenging peer group in the lower grade can provide more appropriate learning than a less challenging peer group in the higher grade.

Other variables that should be considered are motivation or lack thereof, social adjustment, physical size and maturity, grades, and attitude of the receiving teacher. These are of lesser importance than test scores and academic environment because: (1) grade skipping may improve motivation; (2) all studies indicate that grade skipping has no negative effect on social adjustment, and some research has shown that grade skipping actually helps adjustment; (3) physical size, maturity, and grades don't appear to make a difference in adjustment; and (4) although attitude of the receiving teacher appears to make a dramatic, immediate difference, it does not seem to have any long-term effects.

In research on the childhoods of more than 1,000 successful women,[6] approximately 15% had skipped a grade in elementary or secondary school. There was an especially high percentage of grade skippers (25%) among the physicians and orchestral musicians who participated in the study.

In reviewing the variables to be considered for grade skipping, it becomes clear that the most important criteria relate to an academically challenging environment, with all other variables of much lesser importance. It is also relatively clear that test scores are the best indicators for grade or subject skipping, despite their limitations.

You may wonder why it is that so many parents, teachers, and administrators oppose grade skipping when controlled research documents its success, both academically and socially. People tend to base their evaluations of the success of grade skipping on their personal experiences with children who were grade skipped. Almost everyone can recount a grade-skipping story about an adolescent who has experienced difficult social adjustment problems, and they are quick to assume that the problems were caused by the skipping of one or more grades.

Normal adolescents, however, gifted or otherwise, skipped or not skipped, experience developmentally appropriate problems during adolescence. Sometimes they're not invited to a party where they'd like to be, and they usually must cope with rejection by at least one boyfriend or girlfriend. Unfortunately, when grade-skipped adolescents encounter these typical problems, they, their parents, and their teachers tend to blame the problems on the grade skipping. If they haven't jumped a grade, however, the problems are assumed to be normal. Some research also indicated that very gifted children (those with IQs of over 145) tend to have greater social problems than more typical gifted children; thus, the assumption that grade skipping causes social problems is made by adults who are not specialized in the psychology of gifted children.

If you believe that your child is a candidate for grade skipping, find a psychologist who specializes in working with gifted children to evaluate your child. If the psychologist agrees with your conclusions after an assessment has been completed, ask the psychologist to meet with the school administration to make the recommendation for grade skipping. Ask the school to use the *Iowa Acceleration Scale*[7] to guide the decision. This instrument, developed over several decades, guides a child-study team to systematically consider all of the variables that research has shown to be related to a successful whole-grade skip. Sometimes the grade skip may require two steps, with experimental subject acceleration occurring first. After your child has made a successful adjustment to subject acceleration, educators may be more confident of the grade skip.

11

School Ability Grouping

Schools continue to vacillate on issues related to grouping by ability and/or achievement. Homogeneous grouping refers to keeping children with similar achievement levels together, whereas heterogeneous grouping mixes all children regardless of ability or achievement. Homogeneous grouping is sometimes referred to as tracking. Whichever direction the schools take, they appear to be able to cite research that supports their points of view. The reform at any one time seems to relate more to what they've done in the recent past than to what the research data clearly supports. If homogeneous grouping has been used for a while, it appears to be time for a change; on the other hand, if classes have been heterogeneously grouped, schools also perceive it must, again, be time for a change.

Parents also tend to vary in their preferences for ability grouping. However, this variation tends to be less era-related and more attached to the specific group in which their own children are placed. If their children are in the highest group, parents usually prefer homogeneous grouping. If they are in middle or low groups, parents tend to prefer that schools discontinue ability groups. If they have several children who are in two or all three categories, they are very likely to have mixed feelings about grouping.

The attitudes and actions of both educators and parents are logical. For educators, neither homogeneous nor heterogeneous grouping meets the needs of all students. They tend to see only the shortcomings of the system they are currently using; therefore, change seems to signal improvement. We might call this the "grass is always greener" theory. Parents' perceptions based on their own children are also accurate. Gifted children in high achievement groups, in which curriculum is modified, tend to accomplish two grades in one year compared with those who are heterogeneously grouped. If curricular modifications are not made, the gains are much less.

On the other hand, children in middle and low groups are not those making great gains. Although most studies show no effect on the students' self-esteem, loving parents would like to rescue their children from low self-esteem. Children tend to have less academic confidence if they are not achieving as well as others, whether they are grouped homogeneously or heterogeneously, but their lesser confidence is easily blamed on the faulty grouping.

When schools choose heterogeneous or homogeneous grouping, they establish clear priorities for their students. The school that refuses to group children based on academic skills is stating that social adjustment is the first priority, and academic challenge is of lesser importance. When social adjustment is the priority, academic achievement is likely to decline for gifted students and even, perhaps, for all students. As we try to save some children's self-concepts, we may be, in a very global way, preventing gifted students from stretching themselves mentally during a very important stage of cognitive development. Furthermore, prioritizing social adjustment becomes translated by children to mean that peer conformity is the highest value. Recent studies have indicated that adolescent peer groups do not support rigorous learning and that there is a great deal of peer pressure on students who are perceived as "brainy." Removing ability grouping undoubtedly adds to the stress these teenagers feel.

It is hard to predict the educational or emotional outcomes for students who are prevented from developing their mental ability in order to fit socially with their peers. We may recognize the loss only after an entire generation reaches college. Other nations that value achievement are demanding education of their students that is much more challenging. Their students will not slow down to wait for our country's students to catch up.

Although the style of using ability grouping in schools will undoubtedly come and go and change from school to school, parents of intellectually gifted children should keep schools aware of their concern that their children require the opportunity to learn. You may wish to pose the following question to your child's principal or teacher: "Would you like to spend a year going back to learning fractions and decimals or reading eighth-grade literature?" Their answer and your answer to such a question will be "no," yet many intellectually gifted children are in similar positions, relearning skills that they learned three or four years earlier. No one expects an average child to repeat skills after they've already demonstrated competence. Why should an intellectually gifted child be punished with such meaningless learning tasks?

12

Home Schooling and Enrichment

A lack of academic challenge in the classroom sometimes leads parents of gifted children to question whether their children will fare better if they are home schooled. Parents who ponder this question are usually those who have already experienced the joys and satisfactions of teaching their children informally. They feel confident in their ability to challenge and excite their children toward learning. Furthermore, they may be aware that biographies of the eminent in most fields indicate that many were at least temporarily home schooled or individually tutored by a parent, relative, or adult friend. These factors, and frustration with their children's inappropriate education in public schools, convince parents that home schooling provides the best alternative for their gifted children.

In some cases, home schooling is the best alternative. Children who are home schooled for the most part learn skills well. After all, a one-to-one tutorial can be tailored to the specific pace and learning style of a child. There is considerable evidence of the effectiveness of tutorial instruction for all children.

However, there is more to education than learning a body of material. Discussion, peer interaction, cooperation, and competition are all parts of a stimulating learning environment. Children who are home schooled don't usually have as many opportunities to interact intellectually with other students. Although a parent can certainly stimulate and encourage thinking, there is great benefit to variation and peer perspectives.

Perhaps the most serious problems that develop related to home schooling are the pressures that sometimes build between parent, tutor, and child. Teacher and student may become enmeshed in conflict, and with the frequent frustrations, the parent may decide that home schooling is not as ideal as he or she had hoped. When the child is returned to the classroom environment, the problems that initiated the home schooling have often multiplied. Readjustments back to the classroom are hardly ever easy.

Despite some negatives, there are some unusual circumstances when home schooling is ideal, and parents do indeed serve as excellent and inspiring teachers. Some examples include temporary home schooling during a major trip that provides unusual educational opportunities, home schooling of children with extraordinary giftedness, and home schooling of children who live in isolated areas of the country where travel to a school is extremely time consuming.

The home schooling movement has grown rapidly. Home schoolers sometimes form organizations for recreational, athletic, and social activities for their children. Curriculum guides have been created. Although all these add to the positive qualities of home schooling, for most gifted children, it seems logical to make every effort to coordinate home and school environments so that children do most of their learning in the classroom. Although gifted children must sometimes learn to tolerate repetitive material, many teachers are sensitive to the importance of a challenging curriculum.

When children do not find sufficient challenge in the classroom, parents may often provide partial home schooling as an adjunct to the classroom curriculum. They may design, for example, out-of-school experiences that fit well with topics being addressed in school. Thus, students may prepare enrichment projects to share with their teachers and classmates. Sometimes arrangements may be made between parents and teachers for these children to have free time away from some classroom assignments so that they may spend school time on their special projects.

If there are a number of families who become frustrated with inappropriate education for their gifted children and some of them are interested and talented in teaching gifted children, an interest in home schooling can be expanded to the founding of a small private school. Many excellent independent schools for gifted children were initiated in exactly this manner. A small private school can provide the benefits of individualization and challenge. It's recommended that parents do all they can to support and improve their current school, but the parent-led private school offers distinct advantages for children with unusual abilities.

The combination of a positive home-school relationship and flexibility by both parents and teachers usually makes home schooling unnecessary for gifted children. Alternatives suggested in this key and throughout the book may help parents with the frustrations they meet in the attempt to provide their gifted children with challenging curricula. If you are considering home schooling—part time or full time—an excellent resource is Lisa Rivero's book, *Creative Home Schooling: A Resource Guide for Smart Families.*

13

Homework Habits

Homework is a controversial topic in many households. Gifted children vary in their responses to school expectations of homework and study. Achieving children usually study at a desk or table in a quiet place, although some listen to music. However, underachievers exhibit several troublesome study habits. Many are convinced that they study best while lying on their beds with headsets on, watching TV, and reading something over once quickly. Others do homework only after they're nagged, scolded, reminded, and supervised. Even then, they protest and avoid quality work. A third group of children sit with a parent nightly, certain that they can't complete their assignments without that parent's assistance and direct supervision. Finally, some children simply don't do homework or study at all. They may try to convince you that their avoidance of homework is caused by lack of challenging assignments and by boredom. Some gifted children are accurately describing a problem. Many others, however, have simply discovered a way to mislead you. As parents of gifted children who may be in one of these last four groups, you may wonder how your children fell into such bad habits and why other children have better habits.

Good habits begin with an appropriate time and place for study. In determining a good time, you'll need to work around your own family schedules. However, some general rules can guide you in setting both a time and a place.

Children should be allowed time for a break immediately after school to have a snack, enjoy physical activity, or chat. Many children like to watch TV during the break time; however, television places children in a passive mode, making it difficult to move them from TV to homework. It's better to insist that television follow study and homework. Explain to your children that exercise is both relaxing and energizing and is more appropriate after a day of sitting. You may also wish to use a plug lock[8] for your television to emphasize its nonuse before and during homework.

Children are more motivated to do their homework if they have something to look forward to after it's completed. If possible, at least part of the study time should take place before the evening meal, leaving time after study for watching television, reading, or playing games. When study time is too late in the evening, children are often tired and tend to daydream or dawdle. Most children try to postpone bedtime sleep so homework can become a "stay up late" manipulation if it takes place just before bedtime.

The amount of study time varies with children's grade and school requirements. Elementary school children might study from 15 minutes to an hour; middle school children from one to one and a half hours; and high school students from one and a half to two hours per evening. Three or more hours may be required for students in highly academic high schools. Special projects may take considerably longer at almost any grade level. If children say they have completed all of their homework before the allotted study time, suggest that they use the remainder of the scheduled time for reading over material, organizing notes, or extra reading or creative writing. When children have become independent and motivated, there no longer is reason to hold them to an exact time frame. Except for long-term projects, younger children rarely have homework on weekends, so there is no need for Saturday or Sunday study time for most children. That doesn't necessarily hold for high school students who are likely to have some weekend work.

An appropriate study place is equally important for providing an atmosphere in which children learn efficiently. Sitting at a desk with good lighting in a quiet place away from parents and siblings helps children concentrate better and become more actively involved in the material. Some children insist that they can't study without music. If you're preparing them for academic success, it seems realistic for them to develop habits that will help them adjust to environments that will open educational doors for them. (I've never heard of the SAT being given with music blaring or college professors playing music in their lecture halls.) After your children have learned to concentrate in a quiet atmosphere, they may certainly introduce quiet music gradually and experimentally, provided the sound doesn't interfere with their concentration. Research indicates that television interferes even with motivated college students' learning, so parents can feel free to deny TV accompaniment during study time.

There's another advantage to separating your children from family activity during study. Dependent children, who are likely to ask questions before they've tried to solve problems on their own, are less likely to do so if Mom or Dad is physically located at a distance. It's important for your children to take the initiative to work on their homework independently before they ask for help. You should answer questions only after your children have made a determined effort to work out the material on their own. Sometimes gifted children use questioning as a way to gain attention, not because they don't understand the material. Don't sit next to your children during homework time. It's their responsibility to do their homework and yours to take an interest and monitor only when appropriate.

Showing an interest in your children's homework is always important. Reading a story they've written or checking for errors in a composition might be helpful if your children request it. Discussing ideas or quizzing your children in spelling or Spanish is a fine show of support. You can also work with children on special projects; however, it is important that you offer only your guidance, not become overly involved, or they will begin to believe that the project is your responsibility instead of theirs. Furthermore, if the special project is to be graded or entered into a contest, they may feel that your excessive help is pressure and that their grade or award is not honestly deserved.

If your gifted children are underachievers, check their homework on a regular basis to be certain that they're completing quality work; however, don't correct it as a teacher would. If they've done their homework carelessly, indicate this, and let them know that members of your family take pride in their work. If it appears that they're not comprehending a concept, take time to explain it. If you see a misspelled word or an obvious error, you can point it out.

Mothers are often assigned the task of schoolwork supervision, but mothers or fathers can help their children. For boys, it's often helpful if Dad takes the major responsibility for helping with or monitoring schoolwork, especially if the child is not performing well in school. It is important for dads to communicate clearly to their sons about how important they believe schoolwork is. If there is no dad at home, encouragement or support by an uncle, grandfather, or male teacher can be helpful to both mothers and sons.

Parents should always take an enthusiastic and positive interest in their children's schoolwork and learning. It makes a great difference to them!

14

Parent-School Communication

Most teachers become teachers because they want to teach children. They usually care about their students. Now, you may say that you could prove that this isn't the case with some of the teachers who have taught your children. A small percentage of teachers may feel and act "burned out," may not want to teach anymore, never really wanted to teach, or thought teaching would be something different from what they're experiencing. However, the vast majority of teachers want to guide your children toward positive learning experiences.

Parent-teacher conflicts usually emerge because teachers and parents have different philosophies about how children should be taught. Some parents believe that their philosophies are better than those of their children's teachers, and the parents may be right. On the other hand, the teachers may also be right. When there is a conflict of philosophies between teachers and parents, a united parent-teacher front may be destroyed.

If the parents' educational philosophies cause them to encourage their children to do more than the teacher expects, these philosophies probably won't cause problems because the children continue to receive a message of responsibility from their parents. However, if the parents describe the teacher's philosophies as inappropriate, irrelevant, or boring, the children are given an excuse to avoid doing what the teacher expects and this can provide an unintentional "easy way out" for the children. Even if the parents disagree with the teacher, they should not share their perspective with the children because there is the risk that the children will assume they can escape from school responsibility with parental support.

There are several special communication problems with regard to gifted children. Some teachers who love to teach children are not particularly sympathetic to the needs of gifted children. They may even regard the provision of more challenging assignments for gifted children as elitist and unfair to the other children in their classrooms. Furthermore, because most curricula are designed for average children, teachers may assume gifted students know much less than they actually do. Your efforts to describe your children's capabilities may be met with the too-frequent assumption that you are placing pressure on your children. Also, teachers will undoubtedly remind you that there are 28 or 150 other students for whom they are responsible. Such attitudes cause parents and teachers to feel very frustrated.

Parents search for communication methods to help them become advocates for their children. There is no fool-proof way, but here are sample conversations you can have with children and teachers.[9] Be prepared to be positive, patient, and persevering when communicating with schools.

You can try the following conversation when your child comes home complaining about the work being too easy or his teacher giving too much busywork:

Alejandro: Mom, it's been an awful day. All we do is write, write, write. The teacher gives us so much busywork. I know it all already, and I just hate school.

Mom: I guess that must feel terrible. Why do you suppose your teacher gives all that work?

Alejandro: She's just mean.

Mom: Well, when I think of the teachers who gave me the most work when I was a child, I think they did it because they had very high expectations for their students. Even though I complained, too, now that I look back, I guess I really learned a lot. When you think about it, if your teacher sets high expectations, it means that there will not be gaps in your education. That will help you in the future.

Alejandro: Yeah, I guess so, but I sure will look forward to spring vacation.

Mom: You'll deserve that vacation if you really work your hardest. I bet your teacher will realize you're an excellent student and will provide you with some especially interesting assignments.

After having this conversation with your child, you may want to notice if his assignments are, in fact, too easy or if he would just rather be watching TV. If he is indeed unchallenged, it would be good to try the following conversation with his teacher:

Mom: I came to talk to you because I wanted to share some observations about Alejandro. I know you're an excellent teacher, and as his parents, we've made it clear to him that we value your challenging learning environment. Nevertheless, he says the work is too easy and complains of boredom.

Ms. James: You know, there are many smart students in Alejandro's class. We're trying to prepare our students for middle school where they're given a lot of homework. What makes you think the work is too easy?

Mom: Here are some examples of complex work Alejandro's done independently because he's very interested in moving ahead in math on his own. He also says he would enjoy some more challenging science.

Ms. James: This work is actually quite advanced for a student Alejandro's age. You're not pressuring him at home, are you?

Mom: No, I don't believe so. He's doing this work independently. I was only hoping he could be challenged a little more in math.

Ms. James: Thanks for telling me. I'll try to eliminate some drill work and will consider special assignments. I'll also talk to Mr. Genes, his science teacher, about some special projects.

Sometimes teachers deny that any problem exists. When this occurs, don't argue with them. The teachers probably need some time to think about your concerns, and if you press them, they'll only feel that they must prove their case. Be assured that you've communicated and the teachers have heard your comments. Now permit time and thoughtfulness to bring about change.

Suppose your child comes home with stories about negative comments her teacher has made—for example, "Your mom says you're so gifted. I think you're just lazy." Of course, your child tells you this both because she actually feels hurt and helpless and also because she's hoping you'll take her side against her teacher. First, you might ask her why she thinks the teacher called her lazy. Her response will probably be something like, "I don't know," "I didn't do anything wrong," or "She doesn't like me." Your response, in turn, could be something like this: "I know you're not lazy, so you must be doing something out of character in school. I guess you'll just have to prove yourself by working harder, and she'll probably stop calling you lazy. Not only that, I bet she'll like you better, too."

You could remind your child about how hard she worked on an important project or chore with you to encourage her viewing herself in a more positive way. This would actively compensate for her teacher's negative comments, but avoid your alliance with her against the teacher. Reframe the teacher's comments each time your child expresses a complaint, because although teachers shouldn't be name-calling in the classroom, your child's effort and behavior probably require improvement, or no teacher, not even a bad one, would call her lazy.

Although encouraging your child's improved effort and behavior should be your first priority, if you continue to hear that a teacher is using negative name-calling, report your concern to the school's principal. Absolutely do not tell your child of your report, or he will view it as a battle with his teacher and won't improve his behavior. Principals cannot do anything about problems unless parents share their observations with them, nor can you expect an immediate change. However, take the responsibility of communicating respectfully.

You'll feel good if you have encouraged your child's improved behavior and communicated the problem to the appropriate supervisor. Put aside your own anger, and consider how supportive you can be to your son or daughter's educational accomplishment. Challenge the child to show the teacher that he or she is an achiever and a nice person.

You may wonder why so much emphasis has been placed on positive school communication and advocacy for your children. Below is a case study that illustrates the reason well:

Lateesha came to the clinic because she was a gifted underachiever. She was actually to be retained in sixth grade because she had refused to do any homework assignments all year. Her report card showed all Fs, and her achievement test scores had declined. She argued with most of her teachers and was even disrespectful toward some. She was disrespectful toward her parents as well. Lateesha told her psychologist that her school life became terrible after third grade when she came to her new school and that she had been an honor roll student at her old school.

Lateesha's parents reflected a similar story. They had complained to the school board and threatened to have the principal fired because they believed nothing was being done for Lateesha. As a result, Lateesha felt empowered to fault the school for her problems. She took no responsibility because she could easily lay the blame on others. By sixth grade, Lateesha had little confidence in her own ability to reverse her underachievement.

Families of underachieving gifted children who come to the Family Achievement Clinic often blame school for their children's underachievement. It's easy for children who lack confidence to find scapegoats for their problems. Because schools sometimes don't provide appropriate programming for gifted children, it's also very easy for parents to become negative about education.

Typically, teachers are not to blame for the child's underachievement. The problem is usually more complex. Helping parents and teachers to work together is, however, an important component of the reversal of underachievement.

Schools are called upon to be everything to everyone, so perhaps it's not surprising that they can't fulfill all their challenges. Positive, patient, and persevering remain the critical traits for parent advocacy. Respectful and positive advocacy are often effective.

15

Challenge Alternatives for Gifted Tweens and Teens

Entrance into middle or junior high school initiates many opportunities both in and out of school that are not generally available to elementary school-age children. Subject acceleration and grade skipping, described in Keys 9 and 10, continue to be alternatives for some teenagers, but now there are many new alternatives.

Talent Search, which was begun at the Johns Hopkins University Center for Talented Youth (CTY), is conducted in many schools throughout the country. Seventh graders who score high (usually above the 94th percentile) on the norm-referenced achievement tests given in their schools are invited to take college entrance exams [*Scholastic Assessment Test* (SAT I) or the *American College Testing Program* (ACT)]. Students who score above 94th percentile from grades two to grades seven are invited to take the *School and College Ability Test* (SCAT), an above-grade-level test that measures verbal and mathematics abilities. Although these tests are far more challenging than any these students have ever taken, they serve to measure the advanced thinking skills of even very gifted students and identify students who need programs that are more challenging.

Talent Search not only identifies gifted students, it also provides opportunities for a variety of summer programs and a school year accelerated with enriched classes in mathematics, science, literature, foreign languages, and creative writing. The CTY Young Students Summer Programs include summer residential programs for students in second through eighth grades. Three-week residential courses are offered at college campuses in many states. Classes and activities are geared to the ages of the students, as well as to their abilities. CTY also offers distance learning opportunities, as well as counseling for children who are identified by Talent Search testing.

Ongoing follow-up research of Talent Search students has found that participation in the program has been productive and motivating for students. Improved feelings of self-worth, as well as reduced arrogance, for these students also resulted from involvement in the combination of the accelerated curriculum and highly intellectual peer stimulation. In addition, participation in the testing provides practice for students in taking tests that they will again be taking before college admission.

Although Johns Hopkins University initiated the first Talent Search programs, other major universities now provide similar programs in other regions of the country. Among the best known are Duke University [Talent Identification Program (TIP)] and Northwestern University [Center for Talent Development (CTD)]. A complete list is included in Resources at the end of the book.

The International Baccalaureate (IB) is an excellent educational opportunity for gifted adolescents. The IB program provides advanced academic content and also focuses on developing a commitment to personal action. It targets not only cognitive growth but also motivational, emotional, and social growth. The program is becoming more available in high schools throughout the country. There is also a pre-IB program provided in some middle schools.

Distance-learning courses for high school and college credit can be another source of challenge. They are available through many universities and are appropriate for gifted students who may wish to graduate early or take high school courses that aren't offered in their own high schools. The college credit courses are usually accepted by students' own state university systems and may be transferable to other colleges or universities as well. The grades may not be transferable, and students should certainly check with specific colleges to determine if such credits are acceptable. Completing distance learning courses without direct teacher assistance or scheduled classes takes a fair amount of self-discipline, but many students are able to accomplish them either because of intrinsic interest in the subject or because they see it as an important step toward accomplishing an acceleration goal. In some high schools, teachers are assigned to mentor students who are taking such courses.

Several states now provide specialty and residential high schools for gifted students. Some schools, such as the Illinois Mathematics and Science Academy, the North Carolina School of Science and Mathematics, and the Texas Academy of Health and Science, emphasize math or science (see Resources at the end of the book). Other residential and specialty schools specialize in the arts or the humanities. There have always been some independent and public magnet schools that provide an advanced curriculum for gifted students. However, they tend to be concentrated in large urban areas only.

The cost of tuition at private or independent middle or high schools may prohibit attendance by many gifted children. Most schools give some financial aid, however, and highly gifted and achieving children may be afforded these opportunities. In general, financial aid is related to family income, but schools vary in their formulas for providing financial assistance. Some private schools provide specific specialties; for example, the Interlochen Music Academy in Michigan is known nationally and internationally for the unique musical preparation it provides its students.

Difficult decisions face parents who consider enrolling their children in residential schools. Many residential high schools are located on college campuses, and some parents hesitate about sending their children into a university environment at so young an age. The greatest worry for parents is having their adolescents leave home three or four years before they typically would. Although most students make the adjustment well, family life with teenagers can sometimes be just too much fun to miss. Of course, there are more than a few parents who might say this in a directly opposite way.

In some middle and many senior high schools, students are offered opportunities to prove competence by testing out of courses. For students who have had enriched or accelerated summer experiences or opportunities to study in other countries, examinations can be used to provide credit without the drudgery of having to take courses in which they already have knowledge. It is important for students to review and prepare for such tests and to have guidelines about what to expect. If students don't pass the examinations, this confirms only that they may not be as knowledgeable as they assumed; it shouldn't be perceived as a failure. Most students who are prepared will pass such examinations, and there is a real savings of time and boredom for them.

The College Level Examination Program (CLEP)[10] offers examinations for students in at least 30 subject areas. Students, regardless of age, may take these tests at a reasonable cost. Many colleges accept these college credits, although some do not. Students should check with the specific colleges they're considering for entrance.

Many high schools provide another desirable option to gifted students through the Advanced Placement (AP) program, which is also sponsored by College Board (see Resources at the end of the book for the College Board office nearest you). Although students can take AP courses individually, most high schools offering this option actually have AP courses taught by teachers, much like honors courses. AP courses have expanded in number and variety and include foreign language, calculus, chemistry, music theory, computer science, biology, English literature, and composition.

Most courses take a full year to complete, and examinations are given by the high schools in the spring of each year. AP credits are accepted by many colleges. However, some of these colleges accept only a limited number of credits. If colleges accept credits, this can be a cost-effective way for high school students to take challenging courses within their high school environment and get a jump start on a typically lengthy higher education.

Early attendance at college provides several other flexible alternatives for gifted high school students. Some high schools and colleges encourage concurrent enrollment; that is, students may take college courses at a local community college or a local university while continuing high school courses. These courses are usually taken during the junior or senior year, although on occasion, sophomore students with unusual talents have taken college courses. Concurrent courses encourage some students to graduate from high school early and attend college full time. Other students will graduate with their high school class but then enter college at advanced levels. Students who choose to take college courses while enrolled in high school usually receive both high school and college credit for the same course. Some high schools will even pay for the tuition for those college courses. If a student is not satisfied with the college grade, he or she may choose not to transfer it to the college record. If it is transferred to a different college, the second college typically accepts the credit without the grade. Either way, the gifted high school student searching for challenge has the opportunity for early exposure to both college curriculum and environment. Early admission to college, with or without graduation from high school, is an excellent way for some gifted students to enrich and accelerate their education.

Some high schools discourage early graduation and early college admission. Also, gifted high school students who might consider this approach may lose the opportunity for scholarships and honors. The early college entrant must be prepared to trade some of these opportunities for the challenge of college work. If students or their parents have doubts about early full-time college work, the strategy of first enrolling part-time while still in secondary school facilitates their decision-making.

Although many parents worry about sending their children to college at ages 14 through 17, actual research data show that when such children are carefully screened and have been involved in accelerated and challenging programs, most make very successful adjustments. Some profoundly gifted children who enter college even earlier continue to live at home. There is no evidence that students who have entered college early have more problems than other students; however, there is considerable evidence that their eventual adjustment is as good as or better than that of gifted students who didn't enter college early. Although it is true that not all students who enter college are happily adjusted, neither are all students of typical age. In a study of more than 1,000 successful women,[11] many of them entered college at ages 16 or 17, with no regrets.

Parents must explore carefully to determine what college support will be available if their adolescents enter college early. They also should be cautious when helping their adolescents to make this difficult decision. Young people should not feel pressured by parents or teachers to enter college before they are academically and emotionally mature enough to handle the special pressures to which they'll be exposed. Although this is an important precaution, early college entrance for gifted students who are ready for college, and have home support as well, has been found to be very successful.

16

Special College Adjustment for Gifted Students

Gifted young people have some special adjustments to make in college, even if they're National Merit Scholars and valedictorians of their high school classes. The first and most difficult adjustment is to the intense competition in colleges. Some of your children may have already shown strong competitive characteristics in high school; others may not ever have seemed concerned about competition. The latter group may not have shown their competitive feelings because they were easily at the top in intellectual or artistic arenas.

Children exhibiting either set of characteristics may experience a humbling shock when they attend a college or university in which most students graduated in the top 10% of their high school classes. Extraordinarily capable students who receive their first Bs for exams or compositions may suddenly feel incapable of anything or everything. Receiving grades of Cs or Ds, even after they've studied, may cause these students to lose trust in their college capabilities. Although in some ways they continue to believe they're intelligent, in other ways they find their feelings of inadequacy to be devastating. The adjustment to no longer being at the top, or simply to feeling average, can cause gifted college students to "shut down," become anxious or depressed, and avoid classes and studying.

Underachievement related to perfectionism may strike for the first time in college for many of these gifted students. The U.S. Office of Education estimates that of the top 5% of this country's high school graduates, 40% do not graduate from college. Most of these students are intellectually gifted.

Your young adults of college age require your support. They worry about disappointing you if their college grades don't meet the levels of their high school years. Don't be quick to assume the lowered grades are caused by too much partying or inattention (although for some, that is the cause). You may wish to state explicitly that although you recognize that they'll do their best, you understand that college can feel intensely competitive and that most students' grades do not remain as high as they were in high school. Here are some suggestions that can help gifted college students:

➤ Never skip a class during your first semester, no matter how boring or irrelevant you believe it to be. You've paid for this education, so you might as well get your money's worth. The lecture or explanation you miss may become the exam question for which you don't quite remember learning the answer. College underachievement almost always begins with missing classes.

➤ Plan to study at least two hours for each hour of class time, even if college seems easy at first. Colleges recommend this guideline; take their advice literally. Two hours is not only for the "dumb" kids; it means *all* students. Find a study place in a library or quiet room. Dormitories are hardly ever effective study places, unless they are specifically designated as intensive study dorms.

➤ Structure your study time on a schedule or organizer at least one week ahead. Visualizing the time allocated for study lessens the pressure you feel.

➤ If you're struggling with course content, find help *before* you fail. Writing labs, tutors, study groups, and counseling abound on college campuses. No one is going to take you by your hand for help; you must initiate the search, but plenty of willing and free help is available. Even students who receive As in college courses sometimes receive tutorial help.

➤ Schedule exercise time at least three times weekly. Daily exercise is even better. Exercise helps you feel alert and in control and provides an excellent tension release. If you schedule exercise with a friend, you're more likely to be faithful to the routine.

➤ Plan for brief social time daily and a little more on the weekends. Don't overallocate your social time. There is always more to do than you plan for. Weekends shouldn't be used for social life alone. Successful college students study at least part of every weekend. Remember, alcohol, drugs, and study don't mix well.

➤ Find friends who are serious students. The intensity of their study will inspire you to study. Surrounding yourself with friends who are "goof-offs" causes you to feel like you're overstudying, even when you've done minimal work.

➤ Develop and keep regular, healthy eating and sleeping habits as much as possible. Fatigue and poor nourishment only increase your feelings of being overwhelmed.

➤ Many students arrange to work while at college. Although the money may be important, protect your initial tuition investment by prioritizing study time before work. Ten hours a week is enough until you adjust to the rigors of college. If possible, find a job that permits you to explore vocational options or build an experience base for your future career, even if you have to volunteer at first.

Although many students begin college with a commitment to a career, course exploration may indeed cause them to change career directions multiple times. Although parents should feel comfortable about discussing career implications with their children, including insights about their own careers, their children must live with their own choices. College students benefit if they can find mentors who are potential models for careers they're considering. They may wish to volunteer to assist professors or off-campus professionals to understand potential future careers better.

Parent influence can be positive, but parent attempts at control hardly ever work anyway and may justifiably result in parent–child alienation. If you have steered them in an appropriate direction during childhood, you have less to worry about. Even if you have, however, you won't be worry free. Children may choose careers that are impractical, unrealistic, and entirely different from those you might wish. Even if you are disappointed, you should restrain criticism. By college age, these are their choices.

Parents should reserve their right not to waste their money. If children are not serious about studying, they should be encouraged to get their own loans. Their personal financial investments will reinforce their personal effort investments.

Education after high school may be very extensive for gifted students. They may require financial support for eight or 10 years to achieve the high-level goals to which they aspire. Whenever possible, parents can match their financial contributions to student's personal commitments. Students are often sacrificing many years of youthful fun to invest in careers that require heavy personal commitment.

The tensions that surround dependence-independence conflicts during these years may challenge even the most loving parents. Although formal education for these gifted students may feel like forever, their nimble minds will be challenged, and the likelihood of their contributions to society will be enhanced.

17

Career Direction and Selection

Gifted children with very specific talents often find themselves motivated to explore careers that employ those particular talents. Multitalented children, however, may or may not direct themselves to a career early. Sometimes they are interested and capable in so many areas that choosing only one is extremely difficult. Furthermore, differential aptitude tests that help students that are more typical find their career directions may only confirm high scores for gifted students in almost every area.

Further complications of multipotentiality take place when college professors or talent coaches identify the extraordinary skills of students. One high school student, taking college courses on a large university campus, was encouraged by both her philosophy and her computer science professors to major in their areas. Neither professor realized that she was still a high school student, but both were impressed by her superior performance.

As another example, talents in music and science often go hand-in-hand, and two teachers separately identifying these talents may enthusiastically encourage their students to pursue these very different fields. Students with such talents often feel they can accomplish whatever they choose and may thus become even further perplexed.

On the other hand, gifted students may also feel pressures that come from their continued extraordinary performances. These pressures may actually prevent them from taking career risks because they fear they may not be able to continue to achieve as successfully in the adult world. One college student who wanted to be a writer confided that, since attending an excellent writers' workshop, she had discontinued all of her writing. She further expressed her need to do original and unique writing and ended our conversation by indicating a wish that she was not so special or intelligent.

These examples of young adult gifted students encapsulate the issues of multipotentiality, expectations, and pressures to choose careers where they may make unique or special contributions. These students not only require career counseling but also should be receiving help from a counselor who specializes in understanding the pressures of giftedness.

Although some parents may have the background to provide their children with career counseling, other parents have limited experience and cannot provide this guidance. If students don't go to specialized counselors, their friends become the ones they turn to for support. Unfortunately, their friends are likely to be as unknowledgeable about careers as they are.

Whether or not your young adult child is willing to seek career counseling, working in situations where they can observe career mentors will be helpful to them. University professors are often willing to have such students as research assistants for either laboratory or library research. Professionals in business, medicine, psychology, law, and many other fields are willing to share career histories, struggles, and joys with young people.

Biographies from libraries and bookstores may not be as personal a source as mentors, but they include a variety of opportunities for understanding career development routes. Unfortunately, in a society where vocational opportunities change so rapidly, students may find themselves directed toward biography-inspired careers that are already overcrowded.

Gifted students are only partially well-advised to follow their passions to their career choices. This recommendation is often given but may ignore the multiple passions of gifted students and the paucity of positions in many career areas. Several students have shared with me that their passions for singing in choirs not only led them astray in college (too much singing left little time for study) but also provided no foundation at all for the world of work. Aptitudes and intense interests should be tempered by career realities. Even when students finally believe they've found their career directions, interviews with adult practitioners are critical for confirming or deterring their choices.

A rapidly changing society should also encourage students to prepare themselves for multiple related opportunities. It is not unusual for adults to alter their careers several times during their lives. Students who prepare for this flexibility expand their opportunities and choices. Furthermore, intellectually and creatively gifted adults often enjoy the challenge that comes with multiple career directions.

Part Two

Family Issues for Gifted Children

18

First and Only Children

Some special parenting issues affect first and only children, especially gifted children, and can enhance their giftedness; other issues can cause serious problems. Some of these issues make parenting easier, but others make it harder. First and only children are all unique, though, so some of the general descriptors of gifted children do not fit all of them.

First children are only children for at least a little time until siblings are born. Sometimes they are only children for many years. Therefore, they are at risk of being attention addicted and too powerful. With a two-to-one, adult-to-child ratio, they easily become the center of adult attention. If you add several grandparents or aunts and uncles, the attention ratio may be multiplied. It's easy to take one child along to adult social functions at which the child may be the center of an adult audience or included in adult conversations. Parents may treat them as consultants—for example, "Where would you like to eat?" or "What would you like to do tonight?" These children feel equally powerful to their parents, and sometimes, even more powerful. Democracy may begin too early for first and only children. They can't imagine why they require adult guidance when they already feel like one of the adults, and they may not do well sharing attention when other bright children in the family attract the attention of their parents.

If they've been only children for a long time, siblings may feel particularly threatening to them.

There are also favorable characteristics attributable to being a first or only child. First and only children often become very independent. They are frequently good at individual and leadership activities. Because these children are not surrounded by siblings, they may take the initiative to keep themselves busy, interested, and interesting. Unaccustomed to the company of other children, they may not feel as pressured to be part of peer groups and are often willing to take the risk of not conforming to teenage crowds.

You may also wonder what research reports about first and only children. Among the eminent in almost every field, a disproportionately large number are first or only children. The author's *See Jane Win®* study of more than 1,000 successful women confirmed that there were more first children in almost all of the high-status careers surveyed. Also, in studies of IQ and birth order, on the average, oldest children tend to have higher IQs than their younger siblings. To compound the issue further, among underachieving gifted children, more than the expected proportions are only children. There can be only mixed predictions about achievement based on a child being a singlet.

Here are some suggestions that can maximize the advantages and minimize the problems of first and only children:[12]

➤ Be sure to keep an adult life that is separate from your child's activities. If your child resents not being included, remind your child how fortunate she is to have parents who love each other so much that they continue to enjoy each other's adult company.

➤ Don't include your child in adult social functions to which no other children were invited.

➤ Be sure that neither parent includes the child in negative intimate conversation about the other parent, giving a child more adult or more powerful status than a parent.

➤ Don't feel guilty when you see your child playing alone. This cultivates independence and imagination. Choose a regular time each day for your child to develop the habit of being alone. Explain to the child positively that he can choose special quiet activities. Also, explain that you plan to use this time for your own personal interests and activities. Show your child how a mechanical timer works, and explain that the buzzer will signal the end of quiet time. The first quiet times should be short; 10 or 15 minutes may be sufficient. Gradually expand the time to at least a half hour. Your child may actually learn to enjoy playing alone and wish to continue even after the timer buzzes. Soon you'll be able to eliminate the timer. Your child may complain of boredom initially but will initiate activities eventually if you ignore the complaints. With time and opportunity, the activities become rewarding in themselves.

➤ If your child has cousins who are close in age, invite them to spend some vacation time with your family.

➤ If there are no children of similar age in the neighborhood, some taxiing to friends' homes may be required so that your child has practice in sharing adult attention and playing with peers.

➤ Summer day camps or enrichment programs that require shared attention are especially healthy for preschoolers who are only children.

➤ Family camps or conservation and learning projects in which your family participates with other families with more than one child can help your child to keep her special status in perspective and also expose her to variations in family structure—for example, those with many children or with single parents.

➤ Try to avoid overprotecting or doing too much for your child. Although it is difficult to know whether you are doing so, you can compare your involvement to that in families you respect who have two or more children.

➤ Avoid overpraising your child (see Key 26). Too much high praise can internalize impossible expectations for your only or oldest child.

➤ When there is only one child, you may be able to afford more material possessions. Nevertheless, pretend to yourself that you can't, so your child doesn't take for granted the gifts you've already so generously given.

➤ Don't feel guilty if you have only one child. That child can be a special joy to you just as you are to your child.

19

Parenting with a United Front

The term "united front" means that, despite differences in preferred parenting styles, adult caretakers should compromise about each other's position so that the view from the children's perspective is of similar expectations, effort, and limits. Gifted children are more likely to be achievers if their parents join together in a united front. [13]

Gifted children are vulnerable to being included in cross-generational alliances with a parent, grandparent, or other adult against the other parent. Parents who have been encouraged to be open and honest in their communication with their children may actually be more open, even intimate, with their children than is appropriate. They may share with their children or adolescents communication that is more adult than they can understand. The main problem with such intimate and equal sharing is that it confers adult status to the child too soon. Furthermore, verbally gifted children sound so much like adults that they often seem to understand more about life than they actually do.

There is a subtle parent rivalry, hardly ever spelled out in parenting books, that causes problems for families. For the purpose of example, let's examine the traditional two-parent family. Both parents are concerned about being good parents, and because our society is so competitive, this wish to be a good parent can become focused on being the "best" parent. If being the best parent doesn't set up contradictions between parents, then it is likely that they'll be able to cope with the competition they feel and come to agreement on values for their children. In an effort to prove oneself best, however, sometimes one parent may cause the other parent to feel that he or she can never be good enough.

One parent may see him- or herself as best by being kind, caring, loving, and understanding; the other parent may see him- or herself as best based on being respected and expecting a child to take responsibility and show self-discipline. Although each parent sees him- or herself in these different ways, the parents do not see each other in the same way they describe themselves. The parent who sees him- or herself as kind and caring is perceived by the other as overprotective. The parent who views him- or herself as disciplined and responsible is seen by the other as rigid and too strict. They unconsciously decide that their own way is best, and they therefore must balance out the other parent by becoming more extreme. Thus, the kind, caring parent becomes *more* protective to shelter the child from the parent who expects too much. The expecting parent becomes *more* demanding and expects to balance the overprotective parent. The more one expects, the more the other protects, and the more the second protects, the more the first expects. Oddly enough, parents become more extreme in their positions in the belief that they are doing what is best for their children. The outcome for the children is that one parent actually is too strict and the other is overprotective.

If children are faced with parents who have contradictory expectations and if these children lack the confidence to meet the expectations of a parent, they go for protection to the parent who supports "the easy way out." Kind and caring parents, unintentionally, without recognizing the problem they're causing their children, find themselves continually protecting them. When children have grown up in an environment in which one adult allies with them against another adult to find an easy way out, they develop the habit of avoiding challenge. They fear taking intellectual and psychological risks because there is no united support for risk-taking.

To add to the complications in two-parent families, children in our society frequently have more than one caretaker. Sometimes they are reared in families with one, three, or four parents. Grandparents, aunts, and uncles can take on the parenting role. Caretakers may extend to individual childcare providers and daycare teachers. It's very important to the parenting of children that the adults who guide their lives lead them in a reasonably consistent, united way.

The balancing act increases in complexity with three or four parents. Each is desperately anxious to keep their children's love and thus may not provide the best parenting. They attempt to compensate for the other parent in the direction of either expectation or protection. After a divorce, parents are more vulnerable to parent rivalry. They often believe that they can tempt children to loving them by protecting them most, doing too much for them, or buying them more.

It is not unusual for children also to form alliances with grandparents or aunts and uncles against their parents. Grandparents may act on their own rivalry with their children, and aunts and uncles may sabotage their siblings, sometimes unintentionally and other times to act out their own sibling rivalry.

Considering the many caretakers in children's lives, it's not possible to have completely consistent expectations, but certainly among the most critical adults there should be reasonable similarity. If adults are consistent, children know what's expected of them. They also understand that an adult will not assist them to avoid what feels a little hard, scary, or challenging.

Adult-child alliances lead to rituals described as "ogre and dummy" games,[14] where one adult unintentionally portrays the other as a tyrant or as incompetent. Such patterns sabotage and depower a parent, always causing serious harm to children. When adults respect each other's differences and are willing to make compromises in parenting their children, children can be raised in a healthy, positive environment instead of one that leads them to manipulative power and opposition. In summary, if parents can stay united and respect each other and their children's teachers and caretakers, children are more likely to grow up respecting those who have the important responsibility of leading them.

20

Parent Support Groups and National Organizations

Because gifted children are a minority, appropriate education is unlikely to be provided unless there is vocal and visible community support. Therefore, parent advocacy is important to your gifted child's education. Gina Riggs, former Executive Director of the New Jersey Gifted Child Society, points out that "Parents want for their gifted children the same as all parents want for their children: opportunities to learn all that they are able to learn—no more, but certainly no less."

Whether or not gifted programs are available in your school, you'll want to join or form a parent support group. If there are no such programs, be prepared to be positive, patient, and persevering; a challenge is ahead. Indeed, even if programs are available, these qualities are useful as you try to maintain the good components of present programs and add or change others.

Ideally, in your support for gifted education, you want to model for your children your love of learning and the value you place on education. If schools do not provide quality education, however, there is a risk that your enthusiasm for what you know is important can take you beyond advocate so that you become an adversary. Thus, you may find yourself becoming discouraged and even very angry at the schools. Your challenge is to continue to advocate without being so adversarial that you cause more harm than good.

Although you may want to mobilize community efforts on behalf of gifted children, you may accidentally model oppositional behaviors that can interfere with your children's motivation. If your children perceive a negative or hostile attitude toward schools, teachers, or school administrators, they may easily internalize this as an excuse for avoiding responsibility in academic areas they perceive as boring or irrelevant. They may believe that you condone their avoidance of work because you agree with their perspective on the inappropriateness of assignments or curriculum. Sometimes gifted children become openly hostile or passively aggressive in the belief or hope that their parents will side with them against the teacher or school. Furthermore, they may generalize this defiant behavior to other teachers or future school years when they conclude a curriculum is inappropriate or undesirable.

Parent groups can provide many kinds of support to gifted education. Members can help each other by sharing personal experiences and providing encouragement during those times of isolation that parents of gifted children often experience. Furthermore, they can volunteer to help within school programs and can pool their talents to provide unique learning experiences for their own as well as other gifted children. Support groups can also initiate enrichment programs outside school hours. Some parent groups sponsor Super-Saturdays or evening enrichment classes. Fund-raising for student or teacher activities is always helpful.

Local parent support groups can join state and national organizations dedicated to educating and encouraging gifted children. Members can actively lobby and support legislation for educational opportunities. They can serve on boards of education or local school advisory committees. Conferences and meetings provide further opportunities for parents to learn about giftedness. Most major organizations sponsor annual or biannual conferences, and many state associations sponsor yearly conferences. All associations welcome parents.

If parents don't have a local group, state and national organizations can advise them on how to form one and how to affiliate with an association. National organizations usually provide magazines, journals, bibliographies, and other information on services to help you with your gifted child. (Names and addresses of major associations are listed in Resources at the end of the book.) Most national organizations have websites that can provide parents with considerable information. The National Association for Gifted Children includes on its website a list of state affiliates so that parents can locate state organizations easily (www.nagc.org).

Your gifted children will gain much if parents support their needs through positive advocacy. Parents' efforts can benefit all gifted children.

21

Sibling Relationships

Sibling relationships cause concern in all families. Even if there's only one child in your family, this key may apply to you. Cousins who are close in age to your only child may provide both companionship and competition similar to that among siblings. You'll also want to be aware that having gifted children in the family may complicate sibling matters.

Some typical sibling relationships that cause special problems for gifted children and suggestions for dealing with those problems are described here.

Gifted Children with Less Talented Siblings

Gifted children with very high intelligence or extraordinary talents may present impossible competition in their areas of giftedness for other children in their families. These children's unique abilities often require inordinate investments of time and resources to develop their talents and meet their unconventional needs. In the process, gifted children naturally receive large amounts of attention and recognition. Brothers and sisters must be able to admire their gifted siblings' successes but also must recognize that similar levels of success may not be attainable for them. Less talented siblings must use a different measuring stick to evaluate their own abilities, or they may fall into the trap of viewing their own real successes (and themselves) as failures. In the words of one successful sibling of a gifted girl:

> *Once I realized that there was nothing I could do to achieve as well as my sister, I decided to stop competing with her, to do the best I could, and to recognize that what I was doing was really good, too.*

Although this youngster came to understand that he could be successful despite his being a "second-place" student, his realization was not automatic. In addition to rewarding the victories of their most gifted children, parents must also recognize the successes of the other siblings in the family, basing this recognition on each child's individual abilities and effort. As difficult as this may sometimes feel, being honest with children about intellectual differences and limitations is better than pretending that children are all the same. You can also encourage your children by reminding them that their employers of the future will not be requesting their IQ scores but will instead be observing their attitudes, initiative, perseverance, and creative thinking. Furthermore, no matter how intelligent people are, they always find others who are more intelligent.

Gifted Children in Families of Other Achieving Gifted Children

It's not unusual to find that all of the children in a family are gifted. This can be genetic or because of a favorable environment, positive parent and teacher expectations, or most likely, all of these factors. Each child in the family may feel increased pressure to fulfill the expectations set by preceding siblings. The first day of school for the second, third, or fourth child may inevitably begin with "Oh yes, I know your sister. She was such a good student!" This identification may be pleasing if your children believe they can fulfill the teacher's expectations. The early recognition may even produce privileges and trust that otherwise would take longer to earn. On the other hand, less confident children may perceive this early identification by teachers as a threat. They may worry that their performance will be less impressive than that of their older siblings. Sensitive teachers quickly learn to recognize differences between siblings. You may want to explain to your child that "Although Mrs. Jones had Marcus in her class, she'll soon realize that you're also a good worker but that you're a different person from your brother."

Perhaps most important, parents of several gifted children may need to make a specific effort to ease grade pressures for the younger children. Let them know that you understand the special tensions they may feel as a result of the inevitable comparisons with their siblings. Your message can be that all children in the family are expected to do the very best they can and that you'll evaluate their performance individually and not compare it with their siblings.

Gifted Children with Older Siblings of Lesser Abilities Who Are Close in Age

One of the most difficult relationships between siblings is one in which a younger gifted child has a sibling of average (or lower) ability who is older by one or two years. As parents, you may feel an altruistic commitment to "root for the underdog." Although culturally this attitude is very typical, it can place unpleasant pressure on all your children. It can cause parents to refrain from providing appropriate enrichment opportunities for their gifted children out of fear of embarrassing the possibly insecure older children. For gifted children, this strategy produces both frustration, from the reduced opportunities for skill development, and pressure to underachieve and hide their high abilities. The older children feel the sibling pressure anyway. Often they are also less motivated to achieve because of continual assurance that they are not really expected to achieve at higher levels.

A better approach is to reinforce gifted children's achievements, even if this means acceleration to the same grade as the older children. (It's best if the siblings are not in the same classroom.) Also, it's critical that parents reinforce older children's achievements according to their efforts and abilities. As children become mature enough to discuss their differing abilities and the sense of competition they feel, such open discussions help them to deal with their sense of personal worth despite obvious differences in talents, school grades, and academic recognition.

One critical underlying principle should always guide you in decision-making: each child should be provided with the best possible opportunities for intellectual and creative development. A belief in equal treatment in the name of democracy can easily misguide you to withdraw opportunities for gifted children because other siblings are unable to participate. On the other hand, fair treatment provides all children in the family with affordable and attractive opportunities that fit their special interests and capabilities. Treating siblings the same can actually exacerbate the competition they feel.

Children shouldn't feel pressured to be the best in the family in any arena. The world requires many highly capable people, so there are opportunities for all children. Furthermore, although intelligence certainly matters, what children do with their intelligence is much more important. Feelings of competition within the family should be discussed and accepted but funneled to games and other appropriate, less ego-involved outlets. All members of the family require support from each other in a highly competitive world, and encouraging your children to cheer for each other helps them to cope with competition they may indeed feel.

22

Sibling Rivalry

One problem that seems almost inevitable, and probably exasperates parents most often, is the squabbling that takes place among children in the family. Sometimes it even seems that the children can be truly mean to each other. It is frustrating that children whom you love so much can't "just get along together." It feels even more frustrating when they are highly intelligent and should surely know better. Parents find themselves providing endless lectures to their children on how and why they should get along, usually to little avail.[15]

Parents will never be able to make sibling rivalry disappear. Sibling rivalry is a natural response for children who are reasonably assertive. The only time that sibling rivalry disappears is when one child gives the orders, and the other accepts them. Then, of course, the children don't fight. However, if they're assertive, or if one child expects to give all of the orders, most children have differences some of the time. Extreme sibling rivalry is a little more uncomfortable than what typically occurs in families, but parents can take action to minimize the day-to-day rivalry.

First, insist on a little time alone for each child so that they're not always together. If they're always together, obviously they're going to argue more. Separate time alone is also healthy for children's independence, imagination, and confidence.

When your children argue, let them know that you plan to stay out of their arguments unless they hit each other or are too noisy; then you'll become involved. Also, encourage them to talk things out and make compromises with each other. Conflict resolution skills begin at home by children trying to come up with solutions to their problems. Gifted kids often enjoy the reasoning process. Tell them you'd love to hear how they've resolved problems on their own. Explain that you won't mediate or try to determine who is right or wrong. You'll never be able to do this anyway. If your children are hitting each other, then ask them to go into two separate rooms for 10 minutes. If they're merely arguing too loudly, ask them to argue in another room so you won't hear the noise.

Eight-year-old Jean Ann described her new relationship with her big brother this way: "We used to nag at each other all the time, but then Mom separated us every time we'd fight, so we just don't do it as much. It's not fun being separated so much." Most siblings truly enjoy being together, although this may not be obvious from the perspective of their exhausted parents.

Remember: If you mediate, you'll only make problems worse. Each child will try to get you on his or her side, and the fighting will increase. The child you rescue most may be the one who starts the battles. Here are some other suggestions to help alleviate sibling rivalry:

> ➤ A reward system can be used temporarily to reinforce children's cooperative behavior. This works particularly well when siblings are required to spend a great amount of time together—for example, during summer vacation or a long car ride. By dividing the day into two or three sections, such as early morning to noon, afternoon to dinner or evening meal, and evening meal to bedtime, children can receive a point for each time period of cooperative behavior. Siblings receive a point only if both (or all) children are being nice to each other. This point system encourages

their cooperation. The goal is to accumulate a small number of points (10 to 15) toward an activity, such as going out for pizza, going to a movie, or renting a special video. You'll know that your system has been effective when one child hits or teases another and the other one says she doesn't mind because it was all in fun. This is real confirmation of your children's cooperation. No system works forever, but this is effective during particularly stressful times. You and your children can also create your own schemes.

➤ Surprise plans can be used to build cooperation between siblings. When one parent gathers the children together to plan a surprise for the other parent or for another child, then the children become involved in planning toward a goal and feel closer. Alliances with positive goals build children's unity. The secrets of gift giving, surprises, and parties can help unite brothers and sisters and diminish arguing. Special projects or plans for Grandma, Grandpa, an aunt, uncle, neighbor, or friend encourage a sense of togetherness that comes from joint efforts. Parents can effectively use cooperative strategies often to build sibling solidarity.

➤ Sibling rivalry frequently affects children's achievement. Children tend to assume easily that their accomplishments appear more impressive if their brothers' and sisters' performance is not as good as their own. This may mean that your gifted achieving child may be busy graciously (or not so graciously) degrading other children in the family to feel more gifted. Explain to your children that it's nice to have a "whole, smart family," and remind them that achievement by one child doesn't limit achievement by the others.

➤ Most children have feelings of jealousy and should be encouraged to admit them. Teach children to handle these feelings better by accepting the challenge of openly admiring their sisters and/or brothers. This seems to help everyone and can minimize the put-downs. If your children put each other down, don't take sides at the time. However, you should communicate privately your concern to the child who is doing the putting down. Tell the child you'll be noticing his efforts and will give a secret signal when you notice that he is being nice. There's a much better chance of improved behavior if you don't correct the child in front of siblings. Secret signals are powerful.

➤ Although you'll want to encourage your children's differing strengths and abilities, don't make the mistake of considering one child the scholar; the next, the jock; the third, the social one; and so on. Although your intention is to give each child a special place, children hear this as a very competitive message. They feel that they must be the best in the family at something. All of your children can and should be the best students they can be. In addition, some children may enjoy arts or athletics more than others, and all children should enjoy friendships, although some may be more social than others. The subtle labeling of children based on their particular strengths may only increase the sibling rivalry and make all but the scholar feel that they can't be good students.

➤ Don't appoint an achiever to the role of tutor for an underachiever. It will serve only as a daily put-down for the child being tutored. The tutored child may neither understand nor be able to express her feelings of resentment toward the helpful sibling. Children often say they appreciate their siblings' help, but they also say it makes them feel "dumb."

Be sure to give each child some separate time with each parent for sports, chores around the house, or cultural adventures. Although activities including the entire family can be the norm, children who lack confidence should not always need to function in the shadow of more confident siblings. Separate father and son activities are particularly important for all sons in the family, although these activities are sometimes difficult for fathers. Most dads probably enjoy having the more positive and confident son around all the time. Nevertheless, if fathers hope to develop positive attitudes in all of their sons, each son needs to be with Dad some of the time without the other, or one son may always be feeling second best. Mothers are often protectors, so they should avoid the all-too-common mistake of feeling sorry for their less confident boys. Don't be surprised to find that a growing confidence in one son may cause another to temporarily lose confidence. Parents may feel as if they are precariously balancing on a seesaw.

What probably helps parents the most is knowing that if they refuse to take sides in their children's arguments, the children eventually become closer. By young adulthood, they will have learned that it's possible to share their parents' love, and finally, they'll truly appreciate their siblings.

While the principles described above fit well for school-age children, preschool children may require more instructions from parents and parent modeling how to solve a problem. They may also need parents to be more specific and concrete about timing them out when a child is aggressive or mean.

23

Grandparents and Other Relatives

C lose relationships between gifted children and their relatives are important and often inspirational to the children. As parents, you can help your children to value and appreciate their grandparents and other relatives.

Grandparents

When you talk about your parents (your children's grandparents), emphasize their good qualities and refer to them with respect. Disrespect for your own parents gives your children permission to be disrespectful to both you and their grandparents. You will soon regret your negative communications.

Encourage your children to have one-at-a-time, special visits and trips with their grandparents. This permits both your children and their grandparents to enjoy opportunities to know each other without the grandparental responsibility for significant discipline. You may also want to give the children special permission for treats when they are with their grandparents. If you let your children know that there can be flexibility and exceptions when they visit their grandparents, the grandparents, who might provide the treat anyway, won't be in the position of sabotaging your power.

Grandparents may need some written instructions for the general routines to which your young children are accustomed.[16]

If you have some childhood resentment and anger toward your own parents, it's better not to share these with children. Parents' feelings are most likely too complex for even gifted children to understand, and children are likely to resent parents or grandparents and feel caught in the middle. Finally, if grandparents are ill or aging uncomfortably, encourage children to help them and to understand the difficult aging process.

Although children's relationships with their grandparents are usually very special, they can also be quite destructive. Here are some do's and don'ts to share with grandparents to guide them in grandparenting their grandchildren, whom they undoubtedly love:[17]

➤ Do love your grandchild as much as you'd like. You can't love them too much. If you don't express your love, this is a sad loss for you and them.

➤ Do stay in close touch. Telephone your grandchildren directly, or when you're calling their parents, be sure to talk also with the grandchildren. Write letters and send pictures, and encourage the children to do the same. Save the children's letters for them. They will appreciate them when they are grown. E-mail is a great way to keep in touch. If your grandchildren live nearby, arrange regular visits for doing something special. Introduce them to cultural opportunities for which their parents may not have time, or just spend time with them.

➤ Do give special enriched learning gifts. Now may be a time in your life when you are able to purchase a set of encyclopedias for your grandchildren that would be too expensive for the parents of young children to afford. Your grandchildren will remember that you're the one who gave them the special gift, and their parents will appreciate your help. If the children's parents can't manage the cost of a computer or a special camp experience, you may also be able to help with those opportunities. If your own finances are limited, sharing some interesting books or toys from your own childhood may provide an in-depth level of enrichment.

➤ Do share stories about your own childhood. Encourage your grandchildren to record your stories. They will have them forever and will always be able to hear your voice. They will appreciate the past and have a better sense of history. Encourage their questions and observations.

➤ Do play competitive games with your grandchildren. Gifted children may be very competitive, so be sure not to let them always win. They should learn to cope with both winning and losing. Children often recall playing cards with Grandma or playing checkers or chess with Grandpa. Games are also a nice way for informal communication just to "happen."

➤ Do projects with your grandchildren. For example, if you play music, knit, crochet, quilt, sew, work wood, or paint, share these interests with your grandchildren. Sharing skills can have a great impact. It makes the children feel closer to you, and they learn to appreciate your talents. Furthermore, they will always remember that a particular skill was taught to them by their grandparents.

➤ Do read to your grandchildren. Encouraging gifted children to love books is always valuable for them. You may wish to share books from your own childhood or from their parents' childhoods. Listen to your grandchildren read to you, but only if they enjoy reading aloud. Forcing them to read aloud may cause them to feel pressured.

➤ Do listen to your grandchildren. Let them talk to you and tell you stories. Be an attentive audience. Gifted children often love to talk, and other children may not be as interested or may not be at their intellectual level.

➤ Do say positive things about your grandchildren's parents. If the children believe that you respect Mom and Dad, this helps the parents maintain their children's respect. This is good for your grandchildren and for you: they will respect you, too.

➤ Do give your grandchildren a very clear message about education. Tell them how important school and learning are. Ask your grandchildren about their grades and how they're doing, but even more important, ask them about what they're learning in school. Your interest in their learning encourages their interest in their learning.

Here are the don'ts:

➤ Don't spoil your grandchildren by giving them too many material possessions. It makes grandparents feel good to give, but it's not good for children to be given too much. They don't appreciate what they have and only want more. Each time you walk in the door, they expect gifts.

➤ Don't sabotage your grandchildren's parents. Don't secretly tell the children, for example, "Well, Dad is punishing you, but now that your dad is gone, I'll let you watch TV even though he said you couldn't." Sabotaging parents is the most damaging thing that grandparents can do. Gifted children often believe that they're equal to adults, and siding with them against their parents is likely to encourage opposition and rebelliousness.

➤ Don't impose your value system on your children. There may be differences in philosophy between a grandparent and a parent, but the grandparent must defer to the parent's wishes. Grandparents should share some (not too much) information based on their many years of parenting but must leave it up to the parents whether they wish to follow the advice. Sometimes giving your children a parenting book, newspaper article, or tape works best, but again, giving your children too many newspaper clippings may only make them angry and cause them to feel that you're trying to control them.

➤ Don't do too much for your grandchildren. Encourage their independence.

➤ Don't tell grandchildren that they're your favorites. Don't say they're the smartest, the most creative, the best, or the most special. This may make them feel good, but another grandchild may learn about this message, too. By comparison, the other children will feel less favored. Don't call them "kings" or "princesses." They'll internalize these words as pressures and expectations and may expect too much of themselves or become dependent on praise and attention.

➤ Don't talk to your grandchildren's parents about them in negative ways when the children might overhear (referential speaking). Grandparents and parents may say, "He's just a mess," "She's so disorganized," "He's so shy," or "She's afraid to do anything," and the child may hear this and feel negatively labeled. It's always better to talk positively, but do avoid the extremes.

Not all children are blessed with grandparents, nor are all adults of appropriate age fortunate enough to have grandchildren. Informally adopting a grandparent or grandchild may be a way to form a wonderfully warm substitute relationship that provides special joy for children and seniors alike.

Other Relatives

Some children are not only blessed with parents and grandparents who love them, but also have favorite aunts or uncles who adore them. Sometimes aunts or uncles don't have children of their own and may build an especially close relationship with their nieces or nephews. You may wonder what the pleasures and pitfalls of such special relationships may be.

For aunts or uncles without children, relationships with nieces and nephews permit them to experience a kind of fulfillment in a segment of their own lives that they might not otherwise experience. At holiday times, birthdays, and even on special trips, these aunts and uncles may enjoy the companionship of a niece or nephew whom they love and who loves them. For some, however, the joys are mixed blessings because the children may also be reminders that they will not or cannot ever have children of their own. For others, the blessings are only mixed with the relief that they chose not to have the responsibility or burden of parenting. The fun of being with their nieces or nephews only confirms for them that they've made the correct decision. As parents, let your siblings who don't have their own children choose whether to take an interest in your children.

What are the pleasures of these special aunt or uncle relationships? Sometimes aunts or uncles without children of their own can give your children learning experiences, fun excursions, and even gifts that you may not have time or money enough to afford. Because you know that your sisters or brothers are enjoying your children and that your children are benefitting from this special opportunity, you can be pleased for them as well as for your children. Some aunts and uncles are wonderful role models for nieces and nephews and share special skills or interests with them. If you are a single parent, and you have a sister or brother of the same gender as your child (not your gender), it is even more important that your child has an appropriate same-gender role model. An uncle or aunt may be ideal.

There are also risks of special aunt and uncle relationships. Suppose your own sister or brother leads a lifestyle to which you would not like your children to be exposed. Or what happens if your children complain to an aunt or uncle about how hard you are on them, and that relative agrees with your children, taking their side against you? These are major problems for you and your children because you are likely to feel torn between wanting to be a good sister or brother and a good parent. It is important to be a good sister or brother, but most important that you keep the power to guide your children's lives.

Many concerns discussed in Key 22 about sibling rivalry apply to relationships with cousins. Parents should be sensitive about not acting out their own sibling rivalry through their children. Bragging about children's giftedness does nothing to endear your siblings to you, nor does it encourage cousins to love each other. Although most parents know how inappropriate competitive comments can be, hardly any parents seem to be able to contain their enthusiasm about their gifted children's accomplishments. For the most part, relationships with aunts, uncles, and cousins are wonderful connections for your children.

24

Single Parenting and Divorce

The special challenges of parenting gifted children during and after divorce are intensified because gifted children's heightened sensitivities and extended perceptiveness make them even more vulnerable to the risks that attend single parenting. Children in single-parent homes, however, are no longer rare because more than half of the children in our society spend part of their childhoods in single-parent households.

Being a single parent because of divorce, death, or choice continues to be a somewhat lonely responsibility. One advantage of parenting alone, however, is that you may find that you can spend more social time with your children, and their good company can actually relieve some of the loneliness you may feel. Gifted children can become delightful partners for visits to concerts, museums, and resorts. Because of their high-level intellectual or artistic ability (or both), you may thoroughly enjoy exchanges of observations and conversations that are sometimes as stimulating and interesting as those with many adults. However, it is in this specific advantage that there is also risk.

Children who are such good company become easy to take along to adult activities. You may frequently invite them to join you, especially if you lack a significant other and also because of the guilt and expense that accompany leaving them alone with a sitter. Although taking your children along with you may expose them to advanced cultural opportunities that will surely do them no harm, it also exposes them to social and conversational opportunities with adults. Their adult social skills may further tempt you to include them. Even though your children may be easily accepted as adults and as parent partners at adult functions, their adult mannerisms may be oddly out of place when they are generalized to peer social situations. Furthermore, when you attempt to set limits, your adolescents may remind you of their vast experience and insist that you have no right to treat them in so childish a fashion. If you later choose not to include them in attractive adult activities, they may even question your right to leave them at home.

As adolescents who have been given adult status too soon, they may expect you to consult them before you decide to date others and may voice their criticism of your friends of either gender. They've heard other adults criticize; they may consider it their equal right to do the same. Actually, after being "adultized" for so long, they may even object to being barred from adult conversations. Your teenagers, who used to fit in so well, begin to seem very out of place. You'll wonder why and how this negative transition has taken place. It is because teens are not prepared to be treated as adolescents after they've become accustomed to being considered adults.

Now that you're conscious of the risks, you can more easily avoid the problems. From the start, keep a separate adult life for yourself. Join friends for an evening or two a week, and very specifically leave your children at home with trusted caretakers. You need not feel guilty; this is healthy for them. Don't confide intimate details to your children about other adults or a former spouse. The intimacy causes the children to feel close to you but elevates them beyond their levels of maturity. Try to share holidays and celebrations as a family with other families.

Don't tell your children that you will always love them more than anyone or share your bed with them (except during thunderstorms or for weekend morning fun). If you find another adult friend with whom you may choose to share your life, your children will feel betrayed, rejected, and angry at you and your friend. Your children can't be substitutes for your adult partner, no matter how needy and lonely you feel.

Finally, if you are a single mother, try to find appropriate male role models for your children, while recognizing that you're the most important role model for them. If you're a single dad, you'll want to find appropriate female role models.

If you're a single parent because of the death of your spouse, after the grieving period has eased, be sure to share stories with your children about their deceased parent—as spouse, as a child, and as an adult. Even a parent who is no longer living can be an excellent role model for children. Describe your spouse as a good role model, but give your children a balanced description. Your children don't require an image of their deceased parent as having been better than life. Emphasize the positive attributes of the deceased parent, but also let your children know that parents aren't perfect.

Divorce may have brought you to single parenthood, or you may be wondering how to explain to your gifted children that you and your spouse are contemplating divorce. If the latter is the case, it's likely that your children have been anxious about your marital problems for quite awhile, although occasionally children assume that all marriages are in constant conflict and don't anticipate a breakup.

If possible, it is good for both parents to share information about the breakup with their children together. Doing so usually avoids the "blame Mom-blame Dad" game. It's healthier for your children if you can remain respectful with each other even during the divorce process and despite the bitterness that both of you may feel. Give your children specific permission to love both parents.

Divorce isn't always as easy as we would like. Marriages often break up with outlandish and irrational behavior on the part of one or both spouses. Gifted children question morality issues and may feel a responsibility to mediate the relationship or take sides with one parent or the other. There may be almost no way you can prevent a furious adolescent from "snooping" into your adult relationships or lecturing to you or your former spouse about adultery. If you as a parent feel rejected, it is difficult not to encourage your children to see your side of a horrible mess. Children do not need to know all the details of your distressed adult lives. Even if they're gifted and seem to perceive and grasp it all, tell them you can't and won't share your adult issues with them. Of course, you need support for your loneliness and tears; however, counselors, close friends, and sometimes your own parents are your best support. Divorce is an enormous burden that should not be placed on the shoulders of adult-sounding children.

After the mess is over, try to move on to a better life. Don't remind your children when you're angry that their worst characteristics were inherited from the other parent. This causes them to feel helpless to change and angry at you because of the comparison to someone you no longer love. When you arrange visitation, try to keep school rituals and routines regular for children, although admittedly, children adjust to some very strange visitation arrangements. Arrange for clear communication from schools, teachers, doctors, and activity coaches. Schools and churches usually understand their responsibilities for dual communication, provided you make such a request. Keep your children actively involved in interesting activities.

If your children come to visit you and are angry about the adjustment of having to leave the other home, it can make your alliance with them stronger if you say something nice about the parent they've just left. If you're negative about the other parent, they'll probably agree but will feel caught in the middle, and transferring from home to home will be brutal. If you can't avoid being angry with your former spouse when you exchange children, don't talk. Write polite notes instead.

Time and patience will help you and your children adjust to the traumas of divorce and/or single parenthood. Key 25 will help you to introduce your children to new relationships in a blended family if this situation arises.

25

Blending Families

Many gifted children who spend part of their childhoods in single-parent families later join other families to form new family units. When this occurs, the new stepparents become important, and stepsiblings, stepgrandparents, and stepcousins become part of a new kinship circle.

Some of the adjustments discussed in this key apply to all children whether or not they're gifted. However, particular stepsibling combinations or stepgrandparent relationships may cause some special problems for gifted children.

Parenting issues are first priority. It is easy for blending to dissipate into a "my children-your children" brouhaha. Parents need to share their discipline guidelines before they move in together. Compromises and modifications can then proceed more smoothly if the birth parent is the enforcer. The stepparent is initially accepted better in a friendly alliance. Children and adolescents are also much more accepting of a stepparent if they had not been given adult power or intimacy earlier. Parents need to stay united even though it is very tempting to rescue your own child from a stepparent's ire, which may cause the stepparent to become the "ogre" and frustrate you and your partner (see Key 19).

Before the new marriage takes place, prospective parents should discuss with each other their children's personalities, interests, and problems so that they can begin their new families with insights that prevent the unfortunate trespassing on sensitive feelings that can take place early in the new family. The solutions may be as simple as avoiding comments about diet and weight or as complex as understanding that each parent's oldest child has, for example, extraordinary musical talent. What could become a pleasant cooperative venture can easily erode to impossible competition. A child who has a reputation in the family for being best in an arena may experience a difficult personality crisis when another child coming into the family clearly excels or surpasses her in the same talent area.

The competitiveness between the two talented children may easily turn to anger and frustration if both children consider themselves equally talented in music when, in fact, one is much more talented than the other. More worrisome than the anger is the depression or avoidance that can occur for the less talented child, possibly even causing the less talented child to give up music altogether. This shut down can be thought of as a "dethroning" process, whether it relates to having the most musical talent, intellectual capability, athletic skill, beauty, or creativity.

The approach to dealing with this issue of competition is similar to that described in Key 22. Parents must be fair but shouldn't treat the children exactly the same. The children's specific talents should be enriched to the extent possible for each child. However, fair but not equal feels unfair to children who are accustomed to first place. They thus need to be handled gingerly. Explain to your children that competition should stay outside of the family, and that within the family, all children can be talented, even if not equally capable. Remind them that it's normal to have competitive feelings, however. The "whole smart family" can exist even within a blended family. Be prepared to be patient, sensitive, and encouraging. Children require time and understanding for the difficult adjustment of blending families.

As in intact families, when children are closer in age and of the same gender, the competition is likely to be worse. Children may become incredibly angry when they have to share their parent or their "own" room with another sibling. They may also feel guilty about their unwillingness to share when kindness and sensitivity have been an integral part of their personalities in the past. If you don't introduce opportunities to talk about these issues, be prepared for some notable explosions of temper. Sometimes children who are close in age and interests actually enjoy the new close companionship so much that the competition is secondary. Be prepared for either event.

The children's other parents who are outside of the new blended family are also critically important to successful blending and yet are hardly ever in control of their children's new family, and vice versa. It is terribly difficult for mothers or fathers to see their own children relating to another mother or father figure. It is almost as difficult for these parents to see their talented children become only second best in the other family. It exacerbates the pain when they, themselves, have not found another partner and observe the children enjoying their new united family unit while the old family feels painfully empty. Because both parents hardly ever marry and form blended families at the same time, the best way to encourage these parents to be supportive of the blending is to help them realize that they, too, will want support for blending if they remarry. It is also true that children adjust much better to blending families when all parents involved in the process are supportive.

The blending of families hardly ever begins smoothly, but with time and patience, many stepchildren learn to love and respect their stepparents (and vice versa), and many stepsiblings actually become close friends.

Part Three

Other Issues

26

Praise and Positive Reinforcement

Biographical accounts and research on gifted achievers remind us that, as children, they received plenty of praise and positive reinforcement from their families. Typically, they were raised in environments in which parents had positive expectations of them.

It's important to praise your children. Positive comments by parents about their children's accomplishments and good qualities help them to feel good about themselves. Praise helps to build children's self-concepts.

Although it may seem surprising, sometimes praise can also be bad. If praise is too frequent, it may cause children to become dependent upon it, or it may feel meaningless because they've heard the praise so often. If praise is too extreme, it may cause children to internalize feelings of pressure when they feel they can't live up to the expectations established by the praise.

Verbally gifted children readily attract extreme praise. They talk like little "talking machines." Their adult-sounding vocabulary and complex reasoning engage and amaze adults. Grandparents, parents, neighbors, and even strangers in the supermarket are responsive to small children who comment intellectually on skyrocketing prices, the dilemmas of politics, or the state of the ozone layer as if they had in-depth knowledge on any or all of these topics. Some parents discontinue work activities or conversations with other adults to engage in discussions with precocious three- or four-year-olds. Because typically they are astounded by the extraordinary vocabulary, they may punctuate each of the child's statements with extreme praise. They use words such as "brilliant," "genius," "perfect," and "smartest," and comments such as, "I believe you'll cure cancer," or "You'll become president of the United States." Furthermore, if these children are physically attractive, such words as "gorgeous" and "stunning" are also added to the praise statements. If these children also show athletic prowess, parents suggest that it foreshadows the Olympics or professional baseball.

Some parents and grandparents have shared with me their ecstatic comments about their children and grandchildren using phrases such as "she's the greatest," or "he's the most special child." When I explain that praise conveys parent expectations to children, they typically smile and remind me that their little girl, boy, or grandchild really is that special.

The problem is that praise truly does convey adult expectations to children. Although they appear to thrive on this extreme praise as little children, they internalize these praise statements as goals intended to be lived up to as school-age children, adolescents, and adults. If the praise statements are extreme, they are hardly ever able to perform to those extremes. "Perfect" and "brilliant" don't live in the real world of the classroom. Although being "the greatest" and "the best" may be possible in early grades for some children, as the curriculum becomes more challenging, perfectionistic goals become less possible even for highly gifted children (see Key 29).

Children who have received overpraise as preschoolers feel pressured when the praise diminishes. When they enter the world of school, they attempt to do what they have always done as preschoolers. They talk a lot, or they raise their hands constantly, and when they're not called on more frequently than others, they feel attention deprived. Teachers who understand their problems may help them adjust to sharing attention; unfortunately, not all teachers do. Some of them see these children as "pests," and even peers may view these adult-sounding talkers as "weird."

Gifted children who have received too much preschool praise sometimes become school phobic and lose confidence when they enter school. Even more likely, high-energy gifted children—especially boys—who can't cope with their lost sense of specialness may develop behavior problems. Typically, they're seated next to the teacher's desk. They, their parents, and their teachers often feel at a loss and wonder why these children no longer act gifted. Parents, especially mothers, are often blamed for placing too much pressure on their children. For these children, loss of attention and lack of praise cause them to feel pressured and unhappy. However, the pressure these children feel doesn't usually come from over-expectations but from overpraise that they internalized as expectation.

Parents may be able to prevent this pressure problem, at least to some extent. They can praise more moderately and more realistically. They can tell their children they're smart without calling them geniuses. They can tell them they're attractive or pretty without labeling them perfect or smashing. If parents praise children for hard work, good thinking, and perseverance, they'll know that hard work, good thinking, and perseverance are valued. If parents praise them as intelligent, innovative, or creative, they'll know these qualities are valued. If parents comment on their kindness and their sensitivity, it encourages these characteristics. Praise words that are within their control to accomplish are less likely to cause them to feel pressured.

Parents can't necessarily eradicate the extreme praise by neighbors or grandparents, but they can help to interpret it more moderately. For example, when Grandmom calls her grandson the smartest boy in the world, a parent can explain that it's only Grandmom's way of expressing her love, and she really only means that he's a smart child, not the smartest. Parents can't interpret all the overpraise their children attract, but their occasional reinterpretation helps children internalize realistic expectations. A few statements of extreme praise certainly do no harm. It's the constant barrage of overpraise that initiates their attention addiction and impossible self-expectations.

As parents build children's confidence and competence, they can use enthusiastic but moderate and realistic praise. If they praise intermittently and not continuously, it's more effective. Permitting children to enjoy the intrinsic rewards of their activities without becoming dependent on constant attention is more effective. As parents convey their value system to their children, they can avoid burdening them with the impossible pressures of being extraordinary, a genius, or perfect. Someday, children may thank their parents for setting realistically high, but not impossible, expectations.

27

Creativity, Pretending, and Lying

The world of make-believe expands your children's imagination and is just plain fun. Whether you and your children take on the roles of animals or storybook characters or futuristic people, you and they are each exercising your imaginations. Creatively gifted children often exhibit their imaginative abilities early.

Although stories are often read to children, imaginary stories can also be told. These stories can be expanded and embroidered by tellers and listeners. Fairy tales and favorite books can grow new endings or develop different beginnings. Illustrations, three-dimensional projects, and shows that include staging properties can expand fictional characters and plots.

Imaginative play can be part of family time and also thrives when children play alone. Some imaginative siblings or play pairs become involved in make-believe for hours and days. A carton filled with costumes gleaned from Grandma's attic or last week's yard sale adds to the fun. Yard goods left over from sewing projects or old bedspreads and blankets are excellent for habitat hangings. Save cartons from the recycler's truck. Boxes are harder to come by these days, but they serve as effective fortresses, castles, tents, ski mountains, and spaceships. Sound dimensions for drama can come from bells, whistles, old spoons, and pots and pans. Storage space may seem a problem, but consider purchasing fewer expensive toys to leave space for those that lend themselves to more creativity.

Creative children often have imaginary playmates. Don't burst their bubble by not accepting their pretend friends. Join the game of make-believe, although even pretend can go too far:

> *My four-year-old daughter is gifted, exuberant, funny, strong-willed, and tough-minded. She has assumed the identity of fictional characters since she was two years old, going through Maria (Sound of Music), Pinocchio, Cinderella, Charlotte, and Dorothy (Oz). She usually insists on being called by the character of the month and often acts the stories out. Her current person is Carly, her best friend, who is eight. A real person is more complicated. She even insisted on being called Carly when she went back to preschool. She can be very stubborn and demanding about it, although she is basically well-adjusted.*
>
> *Is this going too far? Should we insist on her being called by her real name? This has me baffled! Thanks.*
>
> Baffled Mom[18]

Yes, this four-year-old has gone a little too far, and in my response to this mom, I suggested that she thoroughly enjoy her daughter's imaginary play for a little time each day; however, she should also explain and set a timer for when pretend time is over at home or in preschool. At that time, only real names should be used.

It is very important that imaginative children learn to differentiate pretend from real. If they don't, the pretend begins to invade their real lives. They easily extend stories, fabricate, and lie so comfortably and convincingly that it becomes difficult for parents to know when to believe them. Sometimes even the children become confused. Although this kind of dishonesty is not intentional and is not the same as adult lying, it can easily lead to serious adult problems.

If your child has already begun extending her imaginative story as if it were real, don't accuse her of lying or threaten to punish her. Instead, explain to her (you probably have already) how much you want to be able to trust her and also how you value her imagination. When she's relating a story, ask her to stop briefly and label her continued story as partly pretend if she senses herself going beyond the limits of truth. This permits both you and your child to enjoy her creativity and feel confidence in her honesty. You may even wish to give her an example of how this can be done:

> *Stacy, when you told me that you had three kittens, I knew you were only pretending. I enjoy your stories so much, but it will help me to enjoy them and know you're honest if you tell me you're pretending.*

If you make the mistake of frequently accusing your child of lying, you can expect that she'll automatically lie to protect her first story. Of course, defensive lying can become a very bad habit and serves only to cause your child to feel bad about herself. If you can help her balance the fine line between imagination and lying, you can enhance both her creativity and her honesty. Furthermore, you'll enjoy her delightful imagination within safe limits.

28

Competition at Home and in the Classroom

Competition surrounds children both at home and at school. Parents may find that their gifted children are especially competitive, perhaps because of all the extreme praise they attract and because they frequently function so successfully in school environments. Gifted children internalize early the sense that they should be winners. Also, if the school curriculum is unchallenging, they may further assume that the winning should come easily.

Gifted children who succeed most of the time are frequently shocked when the competition becomes more intense and they've rarely experienced losses. Sometimes they adjust to the new competition. Other times they give up in despair. A distressing percentage of highly successful high school students drop out of college because they were not prepared for the competition in a typical college environment. "Despair" is the exact term these students frequently use to describe the frustration they feel with failure after there have been so many past successes.

Educators found that too many children feel like "losers." As a result, there has been a move away from competition in our schools to rescue children from their feelings of failure. It is true that children who perceive themselves as failures no longer have the confidence required for risk-taking and therefore may close themselves off from further effort. However, teaching children to compete in a society means giving them opportunities for success *and* failure. Winning builds confidence; losing builds character.

Learning to function in competitive environments is not an automatic skill. Although parents want their gifted children to strive for success, teaching these children to compete also requires helping them to experience and cope with unsuccessful experiences. Children are usually spontaneously happy when they are successful; however, sometimes they may be mean or rude to others they deem to be less competent. Furthermore, if they lose, they may feel angry or sad. Sometimes they even avoid competitive arenas unless they are almost certain they can win. The risk of failure feels too frightening to them. As they avoid the many areas they perceive as competitive, they lose opportunities to learn skills and develop self-confidence. Although children cannot be expected to try everything, habits of avoidance can seriously restrict their opportunities. Furthermore, these habits can be generalized to adulthood and narrow career and interest choices. Thus, their home and school environments should provide opportunities for them to test their skills against others who are both more and less competent than they. Contests of skills can teach gifted children how to admire and congratulate others who are winners, as well as to be sensitive to those who lose or fail in a contest.

An appropriate framework for teaching competition at home or in the classroom should be balanced.[19] Competition should not be so intense that children feel constantly pressured. Neither should they feel like they either lose or win all the time. Babying or protecting them from loss is not helpful to them in the long run, even though they may express appreciation at your willingness to save them from stress. If competitive experiences are completely avoided, children cannot learn either to win or lose graciously. Therefore, parents and schools should encourage more and diverse opportunities for competition.

Consider the 4-H model. The many areas of talent in which to compete and many levels of awards invite children to take risks and take pride in their productivity. Blue, red, white, and gold ribbons decorate the showcases of crafts and science projects and plant and animal displays to reward both individual and group enterprise. Beyond the local competition is the county fair; beyond this, youth may be chosen to compete at the state level. Competition has served well for motivating quality production for the many years of 4-H existence and continues effectively to encourage children's learning, creativity, and productivity.

If your children tend to back away from competition or are perfectionistic, it's a good idea to start them with competition against themselves, similar to the "personal best" used in track events. Personal competition at home can include using a timer to improve their time for setting the table, washing the car, or playing a musical piece with fewer and fewer mistakes. Examples of this personal competition as applied to school learning might be to improve speed in math facts by timing and charting time each day. A star or sticker on a chart can be used to mark each improvement over past performance. An example of personal best applied to school grades can reward a grade point average at least one fraction of a point beyond all previous grade point averages.

Group or team competition is the next step and is a very powerful tool for teaching motivation. Team competition at home can include games in which one parent and one or two children compete against another parent and a child. Group competition in school can include informal contests between classes for fundraising, or label collecting at the elementary level, or decorating the halls for homecoming at the high school level. Team sports are the classic training ground for teaching competition. The rules of good sportsmanship are the rules for fair competition and generalize well to both the classroom and life. Some academic team competitions include Future Problem Solving, Odyssey of the Mind, debate, music ensemble contests, Math Olympiad, Junior Engineering and Technological Society, Junior Achievement, Spell Bowl, and the U.S. Academic Decathlon. Most of these team competitions involve elements of individual competition as well as cooperation and thus pave the way for children to risk competing in more personal and independent directions.

Other forms of independent competition include essay and art contests, individual music contests, drama, forensics, talent search testing, scouting events, science fairs, and invention conventions. For a compendium of competitive opportunities, consult *Competition: Maximizing Your Abilities* by Karnes and Riley.

Competition is fundamental to individualism, creativity, excellence, and achievement, and these should be real goals for gifted children, for excellent schools, and for a strong society.

29

Perfectionism

Gifted children are at risk of becoming perfectionistic. You want your children to strive for excellence. Quality work is a reasonable goal, but perfectionism goes beyond excellence; it leaves no room for error. The outcome must be the best. Perfectionism provides little satisfaction and much self-criticism because the results never feel good enough to the doer. Excellence is attainable and provides a good sense of accomplishment. Perfection feels impossible and *is* impossible for the doer to attain, except temporarily.

The pressures of perfectionism may lead to high-achievement motivation or may just as easily lead to problems of underachievement. The pressures children feel to be perfect may originate from extreme praise that they hear from the adults in their environment. They may also come from seeing adults model perfectionistic characteristics, or they may stem from the children's own continuously successful experiences that they then feel they must live up to or exceed. These pressures are only slightly different than the motivation for excellence. This small dissimilarity prevents these children from ever feeling good enough about themselves and precludes their taking risks when they fear the results will not be perfect. They avoid, procrastinate, and feel anxious when they fear they cannot be good enough. They may experience stomachaches, headaches, and depression when they make mistakes or if their performance does not meet their perfectionistic expectations.

In most ways, perfectionists are all-or-nothing people. They see themselves as either perfectly successful or total failures. On the other hand, some children may be only specifically or partially perfectionistic. For example, intellectually gifted children tend to be perfectionistic about their grades and abilities; others may be perfectionistic about their clothes and their appearance; some children are perfectionistic about their athletic prowess or their musical or artistic talent; some are perfectionistic about their room organization and cleanliness; and some children (and incidentally, also some adults) are perfectionistic in two or three areas, although there are some areas that apparently don't pressure or bother them at all.

Perfectionism not only affects perfectionists but also affects those around them. In their efforts to feel good about themselves, perfectionists unconsciously cause others to feel less good. Siblings or friends may feel angry, although they don't often know why. Sometimes they feel depressed and inadequate because they can't ever measure up to the impossible standards of the perfectionist. For perfectionists to maintain their perfect status, they may unconsciously denigrate others. Giving others unsolicited advice seems to reassure perfectionists of how intelligent they are. They're so determined to be impossibly perfect that causing others to feel bad has an unconsciously confirming effect on their own self-concept. So, to balance the perfectionistic child in the family, there often seems to be a "bad kid" or an underachiever.

Here are some ways that you can help your children to avoid perfectionism:[20]

➤ Help your children to understand that they can feel satisfied when they feel they've done *their* best—not necessarily *the* best. Use praise statements that are enthusiastic but more moderate to convey values that children can achieve; for example, "excellent" is better than "perfect," and "You're a good thinker" is better than "You're brilliant."

➤ Explain that children may not be learning if all of their work is perfect and that mistakes are an important part of challenge.

➤ Teach appropriate self-evaluation, and encourage children to learn to take criticism from adults and other students. Teach them how to criticize others sensitively and constructively.

➤ Read biographies that demonstrate how successful people experienced and learned from failures. Emphasize their failure and rejection experiences as well as their successes. Help children to identify with the feelings of those eminent persons as they must have felt when they experienced their rejections.

➤ Share your own mistakes, and model the lessons learned from mistakes. Try to laugh at your own mistakes. Humor helps.

➤ Teach children how bragging affects others and how to congratulate others on their successes.

➤ Teach children routines, habits, and organization, but help them to understand that their habits should not be so rigid that they can't be changed. Purposefully break routines so your children are not enslaved by them. For example, if they make their beds daily, insist that they skip this chore on days when you're in a hurry. If you read to them at night and it's late, insist they go to sleep without reading. Occasional breaks in routines model flexibility.

➤ Teach kids creative problem-solving strategies and how to brainstorm for ideas that keep their self-criticism from interfering with their productivity.

➤ Explain to children that there is more than one correct way to do most everything.

➤ Be a model of healthy excellence. Take pride in the quality of your work, but don't hide your mistakes or be constantly self-critical. Congratulate yourself when you've done a good job by letting children know that your own accomplishments give you satisfaction.

The dilemma for parents is to balance helping children be successful and "good kids" without also causing them to be burdened by the negative side effects of too much pressure to be the best. We want our children to grow up to work hard and take pride in their work but also to feel the satisfaction they have earned.

30

Gifted Children
with Disabilities

Gifted children with disabilities most often receive much more attention for their handicap than their giftedness, both within the family and the school setting. The definition that is used at present to identify children with disabilities comes from Public Law 94-142:

> ...mentally retarded, hard-of-hearing, deaf, speech impaired, visually handicapped, seriously emotionally disturbed, orthopedically impaired or other health impaired children, or children with specific learning disabilities who by reason thereof require special education and related services.

Except for the category of mental retardation, gifted children are as likely to have similar disabilities to those that average children might have. Although schools are required to provide for all children's handicaps, experts in the field of their handicaps rarely have experience or training within the area of giftedness and thus frequently ignore these characteristics unless they are brought to their attention by the children's parents or other teachers.

Although the term "learning disabled gifted" may sound like an oxymoron, there are in fact children who have excellent abstract thinking abilities, superior oral communication, and outstanding problem solving skills but who may also have disabilities in the areas of short-term memory, spatial skills, visual or auditory processing, or visual-motor integration.

Some dependent underachievers show symptoms of disabilities that disappear when they reverse their underachievement; however, these symptoms may affect their self-concept and school achievement. Children who qualify as both having a disability and gifted are often referred to as "twice exceptional." Figure 30.1 can help parents to discriminate between disability and dependence.

Figure 30.1: Ways to Discriminate between Dependence and Disability[21]

Dependence	Disability
1. Child regularly asks for explanations despite differences in subject matter.	Child asks for explanations in particular subjects that are difficult.
2. Child asks for explanation of instructions regardless of style used, either auditory or visual.	Child asks for explanations of instructions only when given in one instruction style, either auditory or visual, but not both.
3. Child's questions are not specific to material but appear to be mainly to gain adult attention.	Child's questions are specific to material, and once process is explained, child works efficiently.
4. Child is disorganized or slow in assignments but becomes much more efficient when a meaningful reward is presented as motivation.	Child's disorganization or slow pace continues despite motivating rewards.
5. Child works only when an adult is nearby at school and/or at home.	Child works independently once process is clearly explained.
6. Individually-administered measures of ability indicate that the child is capable of learning the material. Individual tests improve with tester encouragement and support. Group measures may not indicate good abilities or skills.	Both individual and group measures indicate lack of specific abilities or skills. Tester encouragement has no significant effect on scores.

Dependence	Disability
7. Child regularly exhibits "poor me" body language (tears, helplessness, pouting, copying) when new work is presented. Teacher or other adult attention serves to ease the symptoms.	Child exhibits "poor me" body language only with instructions or assignments in specific disability areas and accepts challenges in areas of strength.
8. Parents report whining, complaining, attention-getting temper tantrums, and poor sportsmanship at home.	Although parents may find similar symptoms at home, they tend to be more sporadic than regular, particularly the whining and complaining.
9. Child's "poor me" behavior appears only with one parent, not with the other; only with some teachers, not with others. With some teachers or with the other parent, the child functions fairly well independently.	Although the child's "poor me" behaviors may appear with only one parent or with solicitous teachers, performance is not adequate even when behavior is acceptable.
10. Child learns only when given one-to-one instruction but does not learn in groups, even when instructional mode is varied.	Although child may learn more quickly in a one-to-one setting, he or she also learns efficiently in a group setting, provided the child's disability is taken into consideration when instructions are given.

It is critical to realize that some children who are truly disabled have also become dependent. The key to distinguishing between disability and dependence is the child's response to adult support. If the child performs only with adult support when new material is presented, he or she is too dependent whether or not there is also a disability.

Asperger's Syndrome is a form of autism characterized by high IQ, very good language precocity and memory, but poor social skills. Most common in boys, the syndrome manifests itself at an early age and has been referred to as "the Little Professor Syndrome."

School programs for gifted children with disabilities should include the same components as do other programs for gifted children who do not have disabilities. Acceleration, enrichment, grouping, and special counseling geared toward their giftedness and high achievement should be added to these children's programs. Although their handicaps must be considered, emphasis should be on the children's strengths and the expression of their talents.

Attention disorders seem to be a frequently diagnosed disability in gifted children. Attention deficit-hyperactivity disorder (ADHD), inattentive or hyperactive type, is characterized by high energy and difficulty with concentration, distractibility, impulsivity, disorganization, and hyperactivity for the first diagnosis, and all characteristics but the last for the second diagnosis.

Figure 30.2 includes the characteristics for the two types of ADHD.[22]

Figure 30.2: Characteristics of Attention Deficit–Hyperactivity Disorder

314.00 Attention Deficit–Hyperactivity Disorder, Predominantly Inattentive Type

A. Often fails to give close attention to details or makes careless mistakes in schoolwork, work, or other activities.
B. Often has difficulty sustaining attention in tasks or play activities.
C. Often does not seem to listen when spoken to directly.
D. Often does not follow through on instructions and fails to finish schoolwork, chores, or duties in the workplace (not due to oppositional behavior or failure to understand instructions).
E. Often has difficulty organizing tasks and activities.
F. Often avoids, dislikes, or is reluctant to engage in tasks that require sustained mental effort (such as schoolwork or homework).
G. Often loses things necessary for tasks or activities (e.g., toys, school assignments, pencils, books, or tools).
H. Is often easily distracted by extraneous stimuli.
I. Is often forgetful in daily activities.

314.01 Attention Deficit-Hyperactivity Disorder, Predominantly Hyperactive-Impulsive Type

Hyperactivity

A. Often fidgets with hands or feet or squirms in seat.
B. Often leaves seat in classroom or in other situations in which remaining seated is expected.
C. Often runs about or climbs excessively in situations in which it is inappropriate (in adolescents or adults, may be limited to subjective feelings of restlessness).
D. Often "on the go" or often acts as if "driven by a motor."
E. Often talks excessively.

Impulsivity

F. Often blurts out answers before questions have been completed.
G. Often has difficulty awaiting turn.
H. Often interrupts or intrudes on others (e.g., butts into conversations or games).

Unfortunately, a fair number of these characteristics are found in many high-energy, high-intensity gifted children. If school curriculum is not sufficiently challenging, distraction, working on two activities simultaneously (for example, reading a book while the teacher is teaching math), misbehaving, or daydreaming becomes characteristic of these children's traditional escapes from boredom, and a child may be incorrectly diagnosed as having ADHD. More information about this can be found in *Misdiagnosis and Dual Diagnoses of Gifted Children and Adults: ADHD, Bipolar, OCD, Asperger's, Depression, and Other Disorders,* by Webb, et al.

Because ADHD is considered a disorder, the characteristic symptoms are assumed by many to signal a biochemical problem that should be treated by medication (usually Ritalin® or Adderall®). The diagnosis frequently removes the responsibility or guilt from parents and teachers who are, in fact, struggling with a strong-willed, high-energy, or difficult child.

It is always tempting to latch on to a "sure cure." However, it is critical that parents and teachers know that all tests for attention disorders are observational, and that there are absolutely no definitive biological tests for attention deficit disorders at this time.

Ritalin®, the main medication for ADHD, is sometimes over-used and misused. One teacher of gifted children reported that half of her students were taking Ritalin® for ADHD. Although Ritalin® may help children focus attention, it is important to know that Ritalin® has established side effects for some children, including loss of appetite, tics, insomnia, nausea, stomachaches, headaches, depression, social withdrawal, and loss of energy.

If most of the symptoms of attention disorders can be controlled behaviorally, medication can be avoided for many of these children. The American Academy of Pediatrics, in an attempt to stem the tide of overdiagnosis and overprescription of medication, has released recommendations to pediatricians for diagnosing ADHD (see Figure 30.3). Some children will continue to need both medication and behavioral help.

Figure 30.3: AAP Guidelines for Diagnosing ADHD in Children Ages 6-12[23]

➤ ADHD evaluations should be initiated by the primary care clinician for children who show signs of school difficulties, academic underachievement, troublesome relationships with teachers, family members, and peers, and other behavioral problems. Questions to parents, either directly or through a pre-visit questionnaire, regarding school and behavioral issues may help alert physicians to possible ADHD.

➤ In diagnosing ADHD, physicians should use DSM-IV criteria developed by the American Psychiatric Association. These guidelines require that ADHD symptoms be present in two or more of a child's settings, and that the symptoms adversely affect the child's academic or social functioning for at least six months.

➤ The assessment of ADHD should include information obtained directly from parents or caregivers, as well as a classroom teacher or other school professional, regarding the core symptoms and degree of functional impairment.

➤ Evaluation of a child with ADHD should also include assessment for coexisting conditions: learning and language problems, aggression, disruptive behavior, depression, or anxiety. As many as one-third of children diagnosed with ADHD also have a coexisting condition.

Behavioral changes include learning to set clear limits for your children, although this may not be easy. Following through without overreacting is helpful. Consistency between parents is critically important. Attention to the positive is also important. There are also techniques for teaching children to help themselves to concentrate and avoid behavior problems. Specific classroom approaches to foster in-seat behavior and withdrawal of negative attention are effective. Negative attention given to children who are perceived as "bad kids" serves only to perpetuate their negative behaviors.

Before you decide that medication is the answer to your child's behaviors and concentration problems at home and school, ask yourself these questions:[24]

1. Do you and your child's other parent(s) disagree on how to discipline your child?

2. Do you frequently find yourself being negative and angry with your child?

3. Do you lose your temper often and then apologize and hug your child afterward?

4. Do you find yourself in continuous power struggles with your child, after which you feel quite helpless?

5. Do you find yourself sitting with your child to help with schoolwork because it wasn't finished in school and your child can't concentrate at home?

6. Do you find yourself disorganized and out of control much of the time?

7. Does your child spend two hours or more a day in front of the television or computer?

8. Is your workload so overwhelming that you have little time for quality parent–child time?

9. Does your child concentrate well in areas of special interest or high motivation?

10. Does your child have sufficiently challenging curriculum in school?

11. Is your child involved in appropriate out-of-school activities for energy release?

12. Does your child know how to function well in competition?

If your answer is yes to most of the first nine questions and no to the last three, your child's symptoms of attention disorders can likely be improved by home and school adjustments. More effective parenting will help you and your child and, unlike medication, causes no negative side effects. Parenting has never been easy, but it is probably more difficult in our society today than ever before. As always, helping parents and schools work with this challenging generation of children may make a great difference and help us to avoid automatically medicating high-energy, intense children. Some children require medication to improve their concentration, but the National Association of School Psychologists recommends that medication be considered only after appropriate home and school interventions are attempted for a reasonable period of time.

All children have learning style differences that should be considered in planning their school and home learning programs. Intellectually and creatively gifted children may exhibit these differences more intensely. Parents and teachers who encourage their gifted disabled children's strengths while providing them with techniques to overcome their problems can guide these children with extreme differences toward self-confidence and achievement.

31

Talent in the Arts

Artistic talent typically shows itself early; however, a three-year-old's outstanding violin performance or a toddler's unusual scribbles do not necessarily predict an Isaac Stern or a Pablo Picasso. According to retrospective studies of artists, the seeds of talent were readily observable early, although parents or teachers rarely predicted with certainty that preschooler artistic production would result in extraordinary adult performance or creation.

Biographies that describe the early childhoods of artists and musicians indicate that there was always a home environment hospitable to the emerging talent of the child. Parents themselves were frequently their children's first teachers and were often creators or performers themselves. Siblings were generally involved in the art form also, although sometimes they exhibited somewhat less talent.

Outside the family, first teachers were typically positive and encouraged the child's artistic talent, rather than disciplinarians or highly critical. As talents emerged, later teachers set high expectations, inspired their students to excellence, and led them to competitive opportunities in their talent areas. Once it was clear to the family that a child had unusual talent, adult attention was usually centered on providing the child with appropriate talent-enhancing opportunities, sometimes at the sacrifice of time spent with other family members. For the extraordinarily talented child, there was a sense of specialness, as well as a drive for intense work in the child's area of talent.

For parents of children gifted in the arts, there are some guidelines found within the biographies of artists. Whether your children's special art form is music, dance, painting, or some other artistic arena, they first require the opportunity to express themselves. If intrinsic interest shows itself, it can be enhanced by your encouragement, support, and unpressured instruction. As your children's talents emerge, increasingly high-level teachers can objectively advise you and your children to understand the extent of their talents. It may be difficult for parents to be objective and critical as the children become further advanced in their specialty areas. However, continuing with only one teacher during the learning years can provide a biased view of your children's talents. Also, as you find yourself making sacrifices of both finances and time, monitor carefully the matching investment of time by your children and the credibility of their talents compared with those of peers at contests, exhibits, or concerts.

Although biographies of those who are successful in the arts tell us of artistic numerators, they do not describe the denominators. Many who were talented in the arts as children and whose parents fostered their talents by both encouragement and personal sacrifice were not successful in the arts as adults. Many, as adults, play the piano at restaurants as a second job, teach small children to play the violin, or exhibit their paintings at small art fairs while doing more mundane work to feed their families. The term "starving artist" is not without foundation. Although all involvement in the arts, including as a hobby or teaching others, can be perceived as worthwhile, it is often a disappointing conclusion to a childhood of devotion and sacrifice. Furthermore, there are gifted flutists who have laid down their flutes never to return to them except with thoughts of depression and anger, gifted dancers who cannot even tolerate visiting a dance recital, and easels and brushes that decay and cameras that rust from disuse and disappointment.

Although most parents value artistic talent in their children, they usually recognize that only limited career opportunities exist even for those with extraordinary talents. Therefore, while parents enrich, enhance, sacrifice, and dedicate themselves to their children's special talents, they must also encourage reality testing and help children to develop fallback interests and career skills. Most of all, their children should not feel the pressured expectations that cause them to feel like failures if they are unable to attain the extraordinarily high levels of performance and competition demanded of the arts in our society. If children are prepared psychologically for the risks as well as the expectations, they are better able to adjust to moving from such goals as soloists or lead actors to membership in choral groups, orchestras, or community theaters. They are able to accept less prestigious opportunities, and if finally, even after all their efforts, they do not qualify as sufficiently talented, they can turn elsewhere for their livelihoods and continue in their talent areas to enrich their lives for their own personal or family satisfaction. They will continue, it is hoped, to appreciate the performances of others with a special depth enhanced by their own investments in their talents.

The paradox of great artistic talent is that it is an extraordinary gift and is very sparsely distributed in any population. Although a lifetime of dedication and commitment is required to cultivate this unusual gift, there are few opportunities for extraordinary artists to achieve great success. Even with the combined talent and commitment, there is no way to predict with certainty that your musically or artistically talented child will be able to attain the heights parents have the right to expect. Perhaps the artist's journey can be compared to scaling Mount Everest—the risk is great, the climb is arduous, and the precipices precarious. Even when the peaks are within view, climbers may not be able to attain them. The climb down is frightening but faster and may even involve life-threatening falls. From the foot of the mountain, the peaks remain visible. When artists have attempted to climb their personal Mount Everests, living in the shadows of the mountain may feel forever frustrating and unfulfilling. However, civilization has benefited immensely from the many artists who have risked the climb to make both small and large contributions. Young people committed to the arts deserve support from parents, teachers, and mentors.

32

Risk-Taking for
Inhibited Gifted Children

Although it is probably true that some children are inhibited from birth, all children can learn to increase appropriate risk-taking. Your first step, as parents, is to remove the word "shy" from all conversations with or about your children. The word often becomes a negative and limiting label for children, and whether you address them directly or talk about them to other adults within their hearing (referential speaking), the label limits their sense of personal control. The more frequently children are referred to as shy, the less they feel they can control the shyness. Instead, assume that your children *will* participate in activities, and stay positive about their participation.

When you notice shy children making efforts to be more social, praise them in a quiet, matter-of-fact way. If you exaggerate your praise, it may cause them to feel pressured about their shyness. You may also want to mention their increased maturity to other adults, preferably within the children's hearing. Here's an amusing case study:

Mr. and Mrs. Brandt had come to the psychologist to talk about their son, Karl, who was highly anxious. They also asked for some advice relative to their daughter, Christina, who, at age three, was extremely shy. The therapist suggested that they consider whether they were commenting on Christina's shyness referentially (within her hearing). They acknowledged that they were, and the therapist explained how to use referential speaking positively. The conversation was then redirected to Karl.

Three years later, Mr. and Mrs. Brandt returned to visit the psychologist. This time it was about Christina. They reminded the psychologist about the suggested change in referential speaking. They also explained that it had been so effective that they now needed help with Christina's too aggressive behavior. Wistfully, they longed for a small amount of her earlier shyness to show itself again.

Not all children become quite as courageous as Christina, but it is helpful for parents to teach shy children some risk-taking behaviors.

Shy children often need to be supported, encouraged, and yes, even forced to become involved in some activities. However, select the important activities, and then be matter-of-fact and firm. Parents may permit children to choose any of two or three activities, but they should insist on their involvement. To avoid power struggles, parents shouldn't get into a pattern of telling children that they should become involved and then permit them to persuade parents to change that decision.

Parents should insist that children participate in at least one group lesson or activity for health, safety, and physical fitness; swim lessons, dance, gymnastics, baseball, soccer, tennis, basketball, or similar sports offer various alternatives from which they may choose. For young children, it is best to just sign them up and not give them choices, but for older children, parents can give them a time limit for making the choice, and then sign them up for the activities they've chosen. Parents should drop them off at the activities, leave, and not stay to witness their agony, and they will make less fuss. If parents ignore the tears, children recover quickly. The activities become routine and will help children to build confidence. Soon they'll be signing themselves up for more activities.

Families can play competitive games at home, but it's not good to let children always win. If they withdraw or pout, parents can ignore the pouts and go on having family fun. If they rejoin the game, they can be included without any special notice to their joining. If other family members tease them about being a poor sport, it is better not to protect them. They'll soon learn to protect themselves by overcoming their problem.

Finally, parents should try to get children involved in group competition. Some examples of group competition are Future Problem Solving, Odyssey of the Mind, music ensemble contests, and sports teams.

As children mature and progress, they'll also develop the confidence to become involved in individual competition such as essay and art contests, individual music competitions, forensics, science fairs, and invention conventions.

If children complain about loneliness problems in school, parents can help children brainstorm a few alternative solutions to the problem together. Parents can practice role-playing conversations for solving the problem with children. They can pretend they're the teacher or their friends and practice giving children possible positive and negative responses so they won't be too devastated if the teacher or children don't respond as they'd like. They need to learn to risk accepting no and to realize that they can't always please adults or peers but, nevertheless, can continue to be assertive.

Parents should be empathic if children are feeling lonely but explain that most other children also experience some loneliness. Parents may even wish to reframe the loneliness as experience for independence. Learning to be independent, and even different, can be very difficult; however, it is a life skill that will help them forever. There are likely to be many negative peer experiences to which they'll be exposed, and they require courage and independent strength to face them. Practicing independence early is good preparation for the teenage years ahead.

The most intense period of peer pressure for children is during the middle school years, and children may feel that they must stay away from other children who may be pressing them to accept values with which they are not comfortable.[25] Although parents certainly should encourage them to invite friends to visit occasionally, they should be careful that the invitation is not mandatory. Parents' anxiety about their children's lack of friends may actually cause children to feel more anxious and may even prevent them from acknowledging that they feel lonely.

When shy children attend middle school, they should be encouraged to participate in extracurricular activities in school. Drama, forensics, debate, and the school newspaper are good for encouraging your children's assertiveness and confidence. Children should be encouraged to participate with groups of children who share their interests. Shy children gain courage when they have interests they love to talk about. Stamp collecting, sports cards collections, drama, art, music, science, computers, hiking, and camping are all areas of interest that can encourage their excitement and shared experiences with other children. Interest-centered summer camps can provide them with friendship opportunities that may continue long after camp is over. Attendance at interest-centered conferences will introduce them to friends of all ages. Letters, telephone calls, and visits keep in-depth, interest-centered friendships alive for many years and prevent the loneliness that shy children may feel.

Closer family relationships often result when friends are not around to distract from family activities. Children should know that they can always count on family interests, fun, and support, and their loneliness will be minimized. As children grow older, they'll find more friends with common interests, and they'll appreciate that parents didn't pity them because other children didn't accept them. It is better that children grow in independence rather than become peer dependent. Although the ideal is somewhere between loneliness and peer conformity, parents can value the strengthening experiences children have by helping them learn to stand up and be true to their values.

Because shy children need to take small steps forward, parents should view these suggestions as a long-range plan with noncompetitive activity involvement initially. As children progress in confidence, more new opportunities can be introduced. It's most important to be positive and focus attention on small steps forward.

For some very gifted children, differences between them and their age mates are so extreme that finding peers is almost impossible. The good news is that beyond high school, social opportunities improve considerably, and children's intelligence will no longer be viewed as a disadvantage. Instead of increasing their inhibition, your children's intelligence will increase their confidence and reduce their inhibition.

33

Creative Thinking

Creative thinking is a type of giftedness that may be specific to certain subject or talent areas, or it may be generalized to all of life. Creative thinkers conclude beyond the obvious, originate or organize unique ideas, and are imaginative. They are more likely to thrive in homes and classrooms in which unusual ideas are valued and encouraged, and to lose confidence in their creativity when they are in environments that are rigid or intolerant of differences.

As small children, creative thinkers may feel confused in classrooms that emphasize speed and correct answers. Their answers may not be immediate or definite. They tend to think in "multicolors" rather than "black and white." Thus, their answers to simple questions are typically more complex, elaborate, or even ambiguous. This may cause them problems in classroom assignments that are directed to one answer, or even in standardized testing where they may overinterpret or misinterpret questions and lose time in the analytic process.

Although some children seem to be born with creative insights, all children can be taught to be more creative thinkers. Creative attitudes and creative thinking techniques should be taught both at home and in the classroom. They enhance children's abilities in whichever interest direction they choose.

Cultivating creative characteristics and attitudes in your children encourages their creative thinking. Research indicates that the characteristics of highly creative children include confidence, independence, enthusiasm, curiosity, playfulness, humor, esthetic interests and involvement, appropriate risk-taking, and a generally high number and level of interests. Creative persons typically feel comfortable in their aloneness and tend to have a few good friends rather than many friends. Their friends are often of varying ages and interests. Creative persons tolerate ambiguity well and may even enjoy it. Here are a few examples of how you can cultivate these creative characteristics:

➤ Encourage your children to spend some time alone. If they are continuously surrounded by friends, they cannot learn to enjoy being alone, nor will they have the time to develop creative interests.

➤ Gifted children may make friends who are older or younger and who have different interests. Accept their unusual friendships (within reasonable value guidelines).

➤ Parents should pursue their own creative interests and share them with their children. They will be role models for creativity.

➤ Value children's creative ideas and products, and encourage their creative attitudes.

➤ Don't worry if you have to move several times while your children are young. Many creative adults moved often during their childhoods.

Creative thinking techniques can also be taught. Some examples of techniques to teach children include analogic thinking, brainstorming (see Figure 33.1), attribute listing, morphological synthesis, idea checklists, synectics methods, fantasy analogy, implementation charting, and visualization. There are many more.[26]

Figure 33.2 is an example of how you can help your children use creative problem solving to cope with a peer problem.

Figure 33.1: Ground Rules for Brainstorming[27]

1. Criticism is ruled out. This allows deferred judgment, which contributes to the creative atmosphere so essential to uninhibited imaginations.

2. Freewheeling is welcomed. The wilder the idea the better. Seemingly preposterous ideas sometimes lead to imaginative yet workable solutions.

3. Quantity is wanted. This principle reflects the purpose of the session: to produce a long list of ideas, thus increasing the likelihood of finding good problem solutions.

4. Combination and improvement are sought. This lengthens the idea list. During the session, students will spontaneously "hitchhike" on each other's ideas, with one idea inspiring the next.

Figure 33.2: Creative Problem Solving to Help You with Friends[28]

Sometimes you may find yourself being teased or hurt by others. Here's a way to solve this problem.

1. First, ask yourself what the problem is. Tell yourself what is happening that you find objectionable.

2. Then think about all your options. Consider all the possible responses you might give to the problem. Brainstorm for ideas, observe other kids' responses, and ask adults for suggested options.

3. Choose the best option, and try it out.

4. Evaluate the success of your trial. Did it work?

5. Determine how you might improve it under new circumstances or whether you should try a different option.

6. Remember that you are usually better off confronting a person or dealing with a problem in privacy. If you try to respond in front of other kids, the person will feel embarrassed, and this hardly ever works.

Books listed at the end of this book (Additional Reading) can lead you to many approaches for teaching the creative process. Many books have been written on the topic of creative thinking, and you will also find much information in your library or bookstore to guide you.

As you encourage your children's creativity, bear in mind that even creativity can become too extreme. Key 35 explains how creativity can go awry and can cause gifted children underachievement problems in the name of creativity.

34

Underachievement

I ntellectually gifted children who do not work to their abilities in school are underachieving. They frustrate their parents and teachers because they are obviously capable of satisfactory achievement. Most teachers, and even parents, would concur that underachievement appears to be reaching epidemic proportions.[29]

Unfinished work, disorganization, excuses about forgotten assignments and homework, a disinterest in most academic subjects, and a description of school as boring or useless are the initial indicators of underachievement syndrome. Other characteristics that may also be typical of these children are poor study skills, uneven abilities, high creativity, lack of perseverance, procrastination, perfectionism, and escapes to books, television, video games, or social life.

Underlying the surface characteristics that these children exhibit are two main characteristics. First, underachievers have not regularly experienced the relationship between their own personal efforts and educational outcomes (internal locus of control). Second, they are so highly competitive that they don't dare take the risk of making an effort for fear they will fail to meet their own too-high expectations.

Underachieving children often have expansive but unrealistic dreams of being, for example, famous, millionaires, computer magnates, or professional football players, but have not learned the discipline or goal-setting required to arrive at those dreams. They make protective excuses rather than taking the risk of carrying out the activities that are necessary to fulfill goals that are more realistic.

Underachievers have a great many bad habits that they have developed to protect their fragile self-concepts. They unconsciously manipulate the adults in their lives, both parents and teachers, in ways that keep them feeling safe in the short run but plunge them deeper and deeper into underachievement. During the time when they should be benefitting from the learning experiences of school, they direct their energies toward avoiding learning. They manage to get parents and teachers to provide more help than they actually need (dependent underachievers), or they try to dominate adults by arguing, debating, and pushing limits (dominant underachievers). Sometimes underachievers combine dependent and dominant behaviors.

Adults (parents and teachers) who respond intuitively to underachievers often find themselves frustrated because these intuitive responses may only reinforce already harmful patterns. Counterintuitive responses are actually more helpful. For example, dependent underachievers, by both words and body language, request continuous help and exhibit symptoms of pressure, despite adults' attempts to relieve pressures. As adults ease their burdens and do too much for them, their school achievement and self-confidence diminish further. In contrast, dominant underachievers tempt adults into conflict. As teachers and parents reason with them, they push limits until they perceive themselves to be winners. Intuitively, adults believe that they must convince these children that the adult's positions are correct. The result is anger for both adults and children. Adults find themselves frustrated and either lose control or give in to children in exasperation. Children continue the "pushy," dominating arguing because they believe that there is a reasonable chance of emerging dominant. If adults become irrational and overreact with threats or punishments, children use this overreaction as a rationale for avoiding the responsibility requested by the adults. Furthermore, in their anger, the children bring their problems to other unassuming adults, who then may either side with them or attempt to mediate the problems, giving the children more power than the initial adult (parent and teacher) who was attempting to guide them.

Dominant underachievers are very powerful but often feel powerless. By adolescence, these underachievers tend to have extreme mood swings related to their manipulative successes or failures. Figure 34.1 is a diagram of these types of underachievers. The children in the diagram represent only the characteristics of underachievement; these are not labels for children. Students in the lower quadrants have more severe problems than those in the upper quadrants.

Both home and school environments contribute to underachievement. Underachievement emerges when children feel they can't meet their own expectations or those of their parents and teachers. At home, contradictory messages by parents (see Key 19, "ogre and dummy" games) ritualize a pattern where the child is searching for the easy way out. In the classroom, insufficient challenge provides gifted children with the assumption that "smart is easy," and at a higher or more competitive level of curriculum that is no longer easy, they feel threatened by the new challenge.

Although the problems that lead to underachievement are complex, the behaviors are learned defense mechanisms; therefore, they can be unlearned. The reversal of underachievement is neither easy nor automatic but is certainly possible. Changes in family and school environments can help underachievers build confidence and become motivated to accomplishment. The flip side of the underachievement coin may indeed be "superachievement."

Figure 34.1: The Inner Circle of Achievers[30]

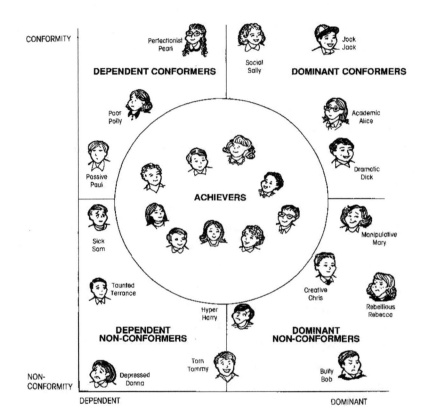

35

Creative Underachievers

Underachieving children are not always creative, and creative children are not always underachievers. However, there seems to be an alarming number of highly creative, capable children who are not achieving well in typical classrooms. Parents of these highly creative children frequently conclude with a certain amount of pride that their children have always "marched to the beat of a different drummer."[31]

Some highly creative children have reputations for causing problems in school. You may wonder if schools are providing appropriately creative programs or whether you, as parents, are causing the problem. These questions may continue to plague you as you see talented but unhappy children. Here's an example:

Bob, a sixth grader, hated school and hated his teacher. He protested on a daily basis about being bored. He loved to read and often read a book beneath his desk when he was supposed to be doing math. Although he was bright, fluent, and verbal, he rarely completed assignments. Despite his dislike of school written work, he took pride in a collection of adventure stories that he had written but wouldn't share with the teacher. He was frequently disciplined by the teacher and had earned a reputation for being the "bad kid" of the class. His parents were engaged in a continuous battle with the school, and his father maintained that schools had not been creative enough for him, either. Dad admitted, somewhat proudly, that he, like his son, had also "marched to the beat of a different drummer."

Highly creative underachievers have some similar characteristics. IQ scores tend to be in the above average to superior ranges (mostly in the 120s) rather than in the very superior range. Creativity test scores are usually above the 75th percentile and by adolescence typically exceed the 90th percentile. The characteristics and interests of these children appear to become more dramatically nonconforming and creative with maturity. IQ scores and creativity scores vary inversely as age increases. IQ scores tend to decrease as creativity scores increase.

Creative underachievers tend to have dominant rather than dependent personalities (see Key 34); that is, they insist on being in control of home, school, and peer activities. If things are not done their way, they may withdraw completely from participation. They seem determined to attract attention to their uniqueness. They usually admit that they enjoy being different, although some will describe loneliness because of their differences.

Creative underachievers, as well as creative achievers, are given a message early by at least one parent about the importance of creativity. This comes most simply by the praise given to children for their creative products and actions. They learn that when they do something unusual, or if they have a funny or different idea, this brings attention. If it is internalized as a personal and positive motivation to be creative, it does not necessarily lead to underachievement. An early indicator of a potential problem is when two parents differ in valuing the child's creativity; for example, Mother values creativity and Father doesn't, or vice versa. The child who identifies with the creative parent is likely to be creative, but if the other parent does not value that creativity, the seeds of opposition and underachievement are already planted.

At the elementary school level, these children may be achievers, although the telltale signs of creative opposition are usually already visible. They may already be voicing complaints about "boring" reading workbooks and "teachers who don't like them." Parents sometimes ally with them against a teacher, justifying their requests for less busywork and more opportunity for individual expression. They may also side with these children on such issues as extending time deadlines for assignments to permit their creative production or convincing principals that too-strict discipline is unfair. Conversations by parents with other adults that take place within children's hearing include references to the lack of creativity in schools or the inadequacy of specific teachers.

The elementary age child develops early the power that comes with an alliance of control with one adult against a system. The school curriculum is interpreted by these children and a one-parent ally as inadequate in terms of interest and creativity. The alliance does not necessarily result in educational harm to the child. It may be productive if the adult and child are realistic in assessing the problem, the curriculum is adjusted, and the child is then expected to conform to these modifications. If the assessment of the problem is not appropriate, or even if it is appropriate and parent and child do not effectively change their attitudes, the child may respond by not conforming to the requirements of the teacher and will feel justified in this opposition. This child then gains too much power in the alliance with a parent against the teacher. The creative underachiever begins a pattern of oppositional nonconformity.

Oppositional young people are faced with impossible pressures. Their internalized value system says to be creative. They translate this to mean that they don't need to conform. By early adolescence, parents are concerned about their children's underachievement and are trying to communicate the importance of achievement. To the child, this message is interpreted as a message to conform. Peers are also demanding conformity for acceptance, but conforming to peers also seems antithetical to these youths' wish to be creative. During these preadolescent years, creative underachievers are typically at their *least* happy selves, sometimes feeling unappreciated by parents, teachers, and peers alike.

By senior high school, opposition is firmly entrenched as a lifestyle. The opposition that began as an alliance with one parent against a teacher has expanded to become opposition against the other parent or both parents and any number of teachers. The manipulated ally varies. The most likely alliance group of all, however, is an oppositional and "different" peer group. The creative underachievers have finally found acceptance by friends who also value nonconformity. They join an alliance with an openly rebellious peer group, determined to be as different as possible from what parents and teachers expect.

There is a fine line of balance between conformity and creativity. When creative children feel so internally pressured to be creative that they define their personal creativity only as what they are against, they risk losing the opportunity to develop their unique talents. If you as parents and teachers can foster their creative productivity and can avoid facilitating escape or avoidance of responsibility in the name of creativity, these creative children can channel their important talent toward productive contributions. Here are some messages that parents might convey to their children:

1. Creativity is a positive word. It suggests that you have good ideas and can make original contributions. It's a quality that our society values.

2. Sometimes creativity is too much. Sometimes it becomes nonconformity for its own sake. Sometimes it becomes a surface message to adults and other kids to simply notice that you dare to be different. Nonconformity and being different become dangerous when kids risk differences that close educational doors on themselves or risk their health or safety. If you refuse to jump some of the boring, conforming hurdles that are part of your education because you believe you should be allowed to engage in creative and interesting enterprises all of the time, you may in fact shut off opportunities for creative careers for your entire adult life.

3. Personal honesty is the key issue. Ask yourself what is truly moti-
    vating your nonconformity. Is it a worthwhile, productive
    motive? Then stay with it. Be strong enough to be independent.

4. Or is it a defensive battle where the issue has become to prove
    you have a right to "do your own thing"?

5. Sometimes creative enterprises are not even nonconformist.
    Try to take a long-range view of your future and how creati-
    vity can move you into the right direction instead of looking
    to creativity as a way of escaping and avoiding the challenges
    of your parents and teachers. Although many highly creative
    persons were not appreciated in their time, many others were.
    If your nonconformity is not valued now by your parents and
    teachers, there is no guarantee that people will value it in the
    future years.

6. Find mentors and peers who encourage your achievement
    and your creative talent. Doors are wide open for hard-wor-
    king, creative students.[32]

36

Gender Issues for Girls

Gifted girls are growing up in a generation of increased opportunities. Professional doors have opened for females in almost all fields, although data continue to acknowledge that a "glass ceiling" effect interferes with women's upward mobility in high-level positions. Some people proclaim that changes in opportunities for gifted women have not evolved rapidly enough; however, most who have experienced these changes are ecstatic at the choices now available to females. Despite the distance to go before society arrives at true equality, girls must be prepared for a different society from the one their parents learned about from those childhood Barbie Doll® play days.

Some main issues in parenting gifted daughters follow:

➤ Girls must learn to cope with competition, or significant doors will be closed to them.

➤ The perfectionism that causes girls to be so self-critical, even in their adult careers, should be modified.

➤ There remains too much emphasis on appearance in relation to attractiveness to males.

➤ Research on the childhoods of more than 1,000 successful women[33] showed that the women considered themselves smart, hardworking, and independent, so these characteristics need to be cultivated in your daughters.

➤ Girls' interest in mathematics and science should be encouraged.

➤ The challenge of combining motherhood with career success continues to create great stress for females.

➤ Professional female role models continue to be lacking in many areas, although there are more now than ever before.

Parents may disagree on whether their gifted daughters should direct their lives primarily toward careers, but hardly any argue about providing educational opportunities to young women that would enable such choices. Parents can help daughters with each of these issues.

Competition

Parents often assume that their daughters aren't competitive, and indeed girls may appear, or even act, less competitive than boys. However, when the 1,000 successful women in the *See Jane Win*® research were asked about the most positive experiences in their childhoods, they mentioned "winning in competition" most frequently. Winning was exhilarating and motivating for these women. They also learned to lose, however, and gained resilience from knowing that losing doesn't mean becoming losers. More than one woman physician mentioned learning about losing by playing on a sports team. Many girls deny their competitive feelings because it isn't "cool" for girls to be competitive or because they fear entering competition where they might not win.

Perfectionism

The perfectionism that so many girls deal with may be an extension of their lack of resilience and avoidance of competitive experiences if they fear not winning. Girls who are permitted to win the moment tears roll down their cheeks are not likely to gain the strength they need to cope with healthy excellence that is rarely perfect. (See Key 28 for suggestions on teaching your children about healthy competition.)

Appearance

Emphasis on beauty and thinness needs to be redirected for girls if they are to view themselves as individuals rather than as recipients of their boyfriends' admiration. Giving young women the message that they are more than their appearance is difficult in our media-driven society. However, the extreme emphasis on excruciatingly thin models, high fashion, and continuous shopping that distracts girls from being thinkers and doers leads them to hide their intellectual, artistic, or creative gifts behind a façade of empty femininity. It makes good, healthy sense to teach proper nutrition, regular exercise, cleanliness, and reasonable attractiveness, given that approximately 10% of college women today struggle with serious eating disorders such as bulimia and anorexia, and many more struggle with weight control and obesity. Both fathers and mothers have a responsibility for giving these clear messages about appearance to their children, without the exaggerated emphasis promulgated by advertising.

During early adolescence, girls physically mature before boys. Their bodies tell them to become interested in boys before boys' bodies tell them to become interested in girls. Therefore, a large group of girls becomes interested in a small group of boys. Girls assess how to attract the few boys and rapidly discover that most boys are more interested in girls' appearance than their brains; thus, a competition develops among the girls. Some gifted girls disguise their brains behind makeup and fashion to attract the few interested boys, and grades and academic interests decline.

In a study of peer popularity that compared average to gifted students, gifted boys were found to be most popular, average boys and girls next in popularity, and gifted girls last in popularity. When the gifted women in the *See Jane Win®* research struggled with issues like being too tall, too short, too fat, or too thin, they tended to immerse themselves in their interests and find their friends within those interests—music, art, horseback riding, drama, student government, sports, religious youth groups, debate, or writing.

Telling girls how beautiful they are doesn't seem to be the answer. Putting beauty in perspective or explaining that beauty goes beyond appearance can help girls most. Also, it's important not to make first comments about a son's dates something like "Isn't she a beauty!" Comments are better that refer to the girl's personality, intelligence, or values, so that young men don't put their entire focus on appearance. Partnerships that are not dependent on appearance are much more likely to last.

Cultivating Positive Characteristics

"Smart," "hardworking," and "independent" were the most frequent terms successful women used to describe themselves in childhood. Most of these women had good academic grades and a good attitude about work. Many considered themselves "shy," "good little girls," "tomboys," and "bookworms." Many of the successful women were less social than typical teens. Quite a few described themselves as "creative" and "leaders." Very few viewed themselves as "troublemakers" or even "fashion leaders." Thus, it seems that it's easier to teach a shy daughter to become assertive and independent than to tame a troublemaker. Girls who are rough and tumble in childhood sports or who seem to read too much may be advantaged in adulthood, perhaps by learning to get along in a male world or by adopting role models from biographies and literature. In girlhood, the women in the study adopted role models that included Marie Curie, Eleanor Roosevelt, Clara Barton, Jo in *Little Women,* and Nancy Drew.

Math and Science

Mathematics ability differences between the genders breed much controversy. The nature-nurture question is continuously debated. Are females born with less potential for mathematics than males, or does our culture cultivate math anxiety and lesser skills in females? Even if genetic differences have some effects, environment can make a great difference, and it already has. The emphasis on math and science for girls has led to improved math achievement for many women, but there is far to go.

Girls' interest in math can be encouraged initially by their parents. If mothers hate math, they need not advertise their distaste to their daughters. Spatial and number games and toys, including cards, checkers, chess, computer games, puzzles, board games, Legos®, and construction toys, should be part of the play collections for both girls and boys. Toys that encourage spatial experiences may contribute to mathematics aptitude. Math problem-solving, whether it relates to planning a new room, shopping, or football yard gains, enhances children's early mathematics comfort. Because mathematics is a threshold skill for many high-status positions, girls who are not confident or competent in mathematics narrow their career choices considerably. Even if they don't choose a career with mathematics emphasis, the society they live in requires a mathematical baseline of skills for almost everything, from completing one's income taxes to becoming active in financial investments.

Motherhood and Careers

Mothers who may have temporarily chosen the "mommy track" or are struggling with the "supermom" goal of combining parenthood and careers can be wonderful role models for their daughters. More than half of the women in the *See Jane Win®* research identified primarily with their mothers. It is important, however, that these mothers communicate to their daughters the satisfaction and value of their careers. Women didn't choose to join the workforce only because they wanted to earn salaries, but also because a career increased self-esteem and was potentially more fulfilling than working only in the home.

Girls need to know that work helps them to feel good about themselves and permits them to contribute to society. Mothers and fathers need to tell their daughters that they take pride in doing quality work and in fully earning their salaries. Although they may be tired at the end of each workday, their weariness comes with the satisfaction of accomplishment.

Mothers shouldn't apologize to their children for their careers. Instead, emphasizing what good role models they are and what important work they do will be more inspiring. Both daughters and sons will take a new pride in parent accomplishments. However, supermoms, or superdads, must also put aside their work and find time for family fun and laughter.

Most mothers miss their children when they're working. They feel some guilt at not being with their children. However, by modeling independence and responsibility, working mothers are fostering their children's independence and responsibility. Children respect their mothers more because they value themselves. Daughters (and sons) also gain confidence by taking responsibility for doing more for themselves rather than depending on Mom or Dad to do for them.

Most women, and some men, too, struggle with the guilt of playing so many roles. Their guilt may not go away, but they get better at managing it if they stop apologizing for it and pat themselves on the back instead. Combining careers with family responsibilities is not easy for women, but they will walk with their heads held higher, and so will their daughters. Women should value what they accomplish, and their daughters will, too.

Role Models

Although girls need good female role models, dads and other men who respect women are also very important role models. More than a quarter of the 1,000 successful women studied identified with their dads, and many were inspired by male teachers, coaches, 4-H leaders, and bosses at work. Many male and female teachers and counselors were pivotal in the success of the fulfilled women in the research.

Career women and those who can combine parenting with their careers can be good role models for their children's female friends as well. Furthermore, parents may be able to introduce their daughters to women friends, colleagues, or leaders in their own fields who can help them inspire their daughters to challenge themselves.

37

Gender Issues for Boys

The world has changed for gifted boys, but not nearly as drastically as for girls. The showing of emotions, the sharing of feelings, and most of all, nurturant parenting are now much more acceptable for young men. In the past, men often felt pressured to hide these aspects of their personalities.

Parents often express ambiguous feelings about sons who wish to play with feminine toys or costumes. A son's lack of interest in sports or a preference for the arts often frightens parents and reflects a societal homophobia. Single female parents frequently feel inadequate because they may find it difficult to provide male role models for their sons, and gifted men struggle to identify how they can be nurturant parents and also model masculinity and success.

Parents mostly require reassurance about the issue of homophobia, or the fear of homosexuality. Although there is evidence that homosexual men sometimes played with stereotypical girl toys as children, there is also plenty of evidence that, as children, heterosexual males also played with dolls, makeup, costumes, jewelry, dishes, and so on. An interest in playing house or make believe is normal for both males and females. Actually, mothers rarely view such play as problematical, but fathers sometimes voice anxious concerns when they see their sons engaged in such play.

Some parents become overly concerned about their sons' lack of interest in sports. When boys or girls are not involved in sports, their lack of interest could be for several reasons. Sometimes their disinterest is related to poor coordination or fear of functioning in competition. It can also be that they are interested in so many other areas that there simply is not enough time remaining in their hectic schedules for involvement in sports. Boys' nonparticipation in sports is also often related to the lack of interest displayed by their parents. It is certainly inappropriate to define masculinity in terms of sports interest and aptitudes. On the other hand, nonparticipation in sports should not serve as a psychological protection for your sons from their involvement in competitive activities or physical fitness. Gifted children often have so many successful experiences in academics or arts that they fear taking risks in areas in which they may not be as successful. If parents believe their sons are avoiding competition, involvement in less competitive team sports may help them learn to function better in competition. For example, swim team or soccer can teach teamwork and competition without putting too much pressure on individuals. Physical fitness activities, such as hiking, biking, swimming, and track, encourage children to develop healthy bodies and strong self-concepts. Backyard sports and intramural team activities, such as volleyball, basketball, and baseball, also facilitate improvement in coordination, health, and sportsmanship.

Although there is little advantage in being involved in sports for typical nonathletic young men, there is great advantage in building physical fitness and great social advantage in learning the language of sports. Listening to conversations between boys and men will convince anyone that some knowledge of sports eases communication barriers. Talking about who won the baseball game is much like talking about the weather; it's what you say after you say hello. Traditionally, this is a male conversation, but word has it that females, too, have increased their interest in sports; thus, a little knowledge from the sports news may ease introductory communication for both genders.

Boys should not be deprived of opportunities to share feelings and express emotions. Some boys do this quite naturally, others are afraid to, and still others would simply rather not. Parents can encourage their sons to express emotions without nagging them. If parents can express their own feelings to their sons and allow them time to respond, modeling and encouragement occur. Parents who constantly remind their sons that they really must express their feelings may unintentionally cause their sons to feel pressured and anxious. If boys have nothing they'd like to say but believe they are supposed to talk anyway, they are likely to feel they are inadequate and that there's something wrong with them. One boy said he wished he could be hypnotized because he felt he had nothing to say but assumed there must be something within him that was special and needed to come out. An atmosphere of openness and honesty encourages expression of feelings for all children. Prohibitions of male tears and sadness or constant nagging about expressing emotions serve equally to close off your sons' (and daughters') feelings.

Providing male role models for nonstereotypical professions should be a deliberate goal, whether there are male role models in the family or not. Elementary age children rarely know male teachers except from physical education classes. They need to realize that men are teachers, artists, poets, authors, and composers of serious music (not only the rock variety). If they see their fathers cook, change diapers, and do child care, they can value the nurturant and creative sides of their own personalities. If only the macho image of males is projected, then gangs and sports become more likely outlets for male identification.

Single mothers can be important role models for their sons, but it is very important developmentally for boys also to have male role models. This can feel frustrating for women who don't have fathers, brothers, or male friends to be supportive to their parenting. Social agencies often assist in encouraging adult males to volunteer leadership and companionship for boys. Support groups for parents of gifted children can also provide an excellent source for effective male role models. Fathers can share their interests and skills with groups of gifted children to encourage challenging experiences for all gifted children, while also being role models for boys who may not have their own fathers.

Most critical of all, boys need to hear and see men showing respect for women as equal partners. This guides them toward respecting and valuing their mothers, their wives, their female colleagues, and other women.

38

Peer Pressure

For gifted achieving students, the middle grade years may be a most difficult time. From about third grade on, there is considerable peer pressure on preadolescents and teenagers to "fit in" with the popular crowd and be accepted by peers.[34] This pressure often seems more extreme for females than it does for males, although most children experience some conflict. On the one hand, they'd like to excel in their activities; on the other hand, they are not certain if their excellence is acceptable to their particular group of friends. They often find themselves torn between developing their talents and hiding these same abilities and efforts for the sake of acceptance.

A survey conducted by Brown and Steinberg (1990) of 8,000 high school students in California and Wisconsin found that fewer than 10% of the high achievers were willing to be identified as part of the "brain" crowd, and students often withdrew from debate, computer clubs, and honors classes to avoid being labeled a "geek," "dweeb," or "nerd."[35] The percentage was even lower for females than for males. None of the high-achieving African-Americans surveyed in the Brown and Steinberg study were willing to be considered part of the "brain" crowd. Peer pressure may indeed be even more difficult for disadvantaged children.

Special vocabulary that labels students who appear too studious has varied through generations. "Brain," "nerd," "brainiac," "schoolboy (or girl)," "bookie," and "geek" are some of the uncomplimentary terms used to describe serious students who don't fit in with the popular crowd. African-American youth who study may be teased as "acting white," and Native-Americans are sometimes called "apples"—red on the outside and white on the inside. These terms can cause a good student to develop a high-risk behavior. Preadolescents may be teased cruelly and even physically abused by groups of other students who do not accept the personality and interest differences of those who are serious about learning and who seem to care only a little about social life. Serious students often feel isolated and unacceptably different. Here is an example:[36]

> *One symphony orchestra player recalled being teased mercilessly for two years. She returned home crying every day when kids called her "brainiac" and "hairy legs" because she loved classical music, was an excellent student, and wasn't as interested in clothes and makeup as her peers. She finally found close friends and self-esteem at music camp and youth symphony orchestras during her high school years.*

Girls who are extremely attractive and boys who are excellent athletes sometimes have enough status to manage both to excel and fit in. However, because teenagers rarely have a great deal of social confidence, hiding one's talents is a fairly frequent behavior. Some children copy, cheat, and are defiant to fit in with friends who are doing the same. Children's problems can become much more serious as they lose skills and academic confidence.

Typically, parents and teachers are very concerned about their children's social adjustment; perhaps they're overconcerned. Some often become anxious if their children don't have friends or aren't popular; others brag about their children's social successes. Parents and teachers discuss social issues frequently, either with their children or students or with other adults within their children's hearing, sending messages that social acceptance is a high priority. Here are some examples:

➤ Most teachers or administrators, when consulted about possible grade skipping for highly gifted children, first ask about the social adjustment involved in such a decision. Parents and teachers may actually use concerns about social adjustment as a basis for not providing academic challenge. Social adjustment seems to be their number one priority.

➤ If children play alone or have only a few friends, both teachers and parents tend to encourage them to join others or invite friends to their homes, almost as if they fear that children who are not popular will not be successful.

➤ Parents and teachers continuously redirect independent activities to social activities and praise the more social children in the family or in the class.

➤ Parents often say repeatedly that they don't want to move to a new city because their children will lose their friends, or they don't want to move to the country because they might be away from friends. They tend to want to be sure there are friends available at all times for their children, as if their children might suffer if they live away from other children.

Peer pressure against learning is a very serious problem in our country. Although it is not good for children to be without friends, childhood years are crucial for teaching them a value system that surely includes honesty and achievement. Parents should not "wimp out" and must let them know early and often that everyone has to go it alone at times in life. It is more important to stand tall and know that they are living by a standard of excellence and integrity than to conform to a peer standard that in the long haul will cause problems. Let children know that it's sometimes all right to walk the school halls alone because this will equip them to be strong.

Parents can't prevent their children from feeling peer pressure in many middle schools unless they encourage their children to

conform to an anti-learning standard, which most parents don't
want to do. This is an opportunity to give children a powerful
message about independence and moral strength. Although it is
difficult for parents to watch children struggle to maintain values
of integrity, honesty, individuality, and love of learning, these
values will begin to pay off for them in only a few more years.
Here are some humorous messages that teachers and counselors
have shared with me:

➤ Explain that the nerds of today will own the Lamborghinis
of tomorrow.

➤ Explain that after grade 12, no one cares who was popular
in middle or high school.

➤ Try this "what do you call" joke:

Counselor: What do you call a student who studies
hard, talks to the teacher after the class, does
extra work, does more than expected, and
wants to do his or her schoolwork?

Student: Nerd, brain, geek.

Counselor: What do you call adults who work hard at
their jobs, do more than expected, want to
meet high standards, and are interested in
their work?

Student: Gee, I don't know.

Counselor: You call them "boss."

When parents make social adjustment the highest priority,
they are also unintentionally giving a message to conform socially.
Their children may be the first to get involved in drinking at parties because they want to fit in and are worried about popularity.

Parents should let children know that it will pay off to be
strong despite peer pressure. They can help them search out other
students who share similar interests so that they don't feel so alone.

They can encourage children's involvement in positive school activities in which they can share fun learning with other students—such activities as band, drama, forensics, computer club, school newspaper, and Future Problem Solving. Children's positive involvement will help them through the peer-pressured days of middle and high school.

This is also an important time for family support. Family trips and activities that interest tweens or teens can lessen their loneliness. Involvement in summer or weekend programs for gifted teens can help them find like-minded peers. The website for the National Association for Gifted Children (www.nagc.org) provides a list of such programs in many interest areas.

Usually, by eleventh grade, the negative peer pressure diminishes, and the academic goals parents have worked so hard to encourage in their children are respected by their peers. By the time they get to college, the nerds and the popular students intermingle. Gifted students in college are not destined to wear "I was a geek in high school" on their foreheads. Nerdiness will be forgotten, and children's academic achievement will open doors to their futures.

39

Grade Pressures and Tension

All children receive some forms of evaluation and feedback from their teachers about their school progress. The communication that describes children's school progress is usually shared directly with parents (except at the college level) in the form of report cards. Although grades are not the only source of pressure for intellectually gifted children, they can certainly cause tension for these children despite their excellent capabilities. Small amounts of tension are, of course, not harmful and are indicators only of reasonable motivation. It is when tensions cause such symptoms as nail biting, headaches, stomachaches, or generalized anxiety that clear indicators of problems present themselves. Often the children who exhibit these tensions, in fact, have good grades, although that is not always the case. Furthermore, when parents observe their children's tension symptoms, they may even feel guilty because they believe that they are causing their children's feelings of pressure.

Sometimes parents can pressure their children by overpraise, rewards, and excitement about their children's grades. Of course, it is appropriate to show enthusiasm for high grades, or children will believe that their grades don't matter to their parents. However, continuous all-A report cards can cause children to feel that these are the only acceptable report cards unless parents temper their excitement with explanations to their children. After all, an all-A report card leaves no room for improvement but much reason to fear lower grades in the future. It is unlikely to cause pressure in the elementary grades, but as curriculum becomes more complex and competition increases, gifted children may actually fear receiving their first Bs.

Parents' discussion with their children about report card grades, the content of their children's learning, and the progress in their efforts permits parents to communicate their important concerns about learning and effort. These discussions can also relay the message to children that challenge involves learning from mistakes and that the curriculum and assignments will become increasingly difficult as students advance in grades. Parents need to guard against overreaction to either excellent or poor grades. Rewards and punishments for grades do little to motivate children. Joint problem-solving strategies are much more effective.

When parents respond to their children's tensions concerning grades with "grades don't count as long as you're learning," they may be initiating a difficult set of problems. Grades do count for college scholarships, honors, and for opening up many other educational opportunities for your children. It is too easy for your children to take literally any lack of concern for their grades. Gifted children also often assume that they should learn only that which interests them. Although parents should certainly encourage the pursuit of their children's interests, children also need to be required to meet general academic expectations. Parents often become confused in their messages because they want to avoid pressuring their children.

Grades count; however, they certainly aren't all- important. "Effort," "initiative," "attitude," and "interests" are terms that can guide your children along a balanced and motivated pathway.

Parents should encourage their children to talk through their grade concerns rather than build internal tensions. If children don't initiate the conversations, parents should; otherwise, children may make assumptions about parents' expectations that are unfair to themselves and to parents.

A balance of physical exercise and recreational activities will help children to cope with physical tensions. If children are showing extreme signs of pressure, counselors may help them to understand their feelings. They may also teach them relaxation exercises or use hypnotherapy or biofeedback to teach them to cope with pressures.

Sometimes children exhibit symptoms of tension when they are not even working to their abilities in school. Assignments that have not been turned in, unwritten term papers, and procrastination may cause children to feel more tension than when they are actually working at their assignments. Even intellectually gifted children can feel overwhelmed by thoughts of what they believe they are supposed to accomplish but feel unable to. They easily set their goals impossibly high. Reassuring them that they will be able to complete an A+ paper may only backfire and cause them to feel even more pressure. If children feel overwhelmed by long-term assignments, it's best initially to help them break up their projects into shorter daily assignments so that they can monitor their steps of progress and even share them with you.

Students who accomplish much in our society do experience tension and pressure at many junctions. Parents can't protect them from these pressures, but they can help to place them in perspective. Furthermore, it's quite important that parents not add unnecessary unrealistic pressures to those that their gifted children may already feel. Parents in general try hard not to pressure their children, but sometimes, in the excitement of their gifted children's accomplishments, it is difficult not to set continuously higher expectations. Parents who conscientiously try to keep good communication with their children are more likely to be sensitive to when they need to modify expectations to assist children in feeling motivated without feeling unreasonable pressure.

40

Computers and the Internet

Many gifted children are attracted by computer technology and the Internet. For now and the future, the expanding role of technology will provide many high-level career positions, so the attraction to technology is likely to pay off in challenging and interesting careers. It is true that the Internet has attracted many gifted "computer geeks" who struggled with social life in middle and high school.

Computers have attracted many more boys than girls, probably because of the vast market of boy-oriented computer games that include sports and violence. Parents should encourage their daughters' computer use as well, and computer companies should be pressed to develop adventurous computer games for girls. Although the author's research on computer use by gender indicated middle grade boys spent more time on games than girls, it also found that girls spent more time on e-mail and the Internet than boys.[37]

Computer games and learning opportunities can be introduced during preschool years. Many three-year-olds find computer screens fascinating. Like television, however, too much time in front of computers is inappropriate. Preschoolers can be taught learning skills through interaction with computers, but not social skills. Computers are definitely not good babysitters.

By school age, children can expand their learning from computer games to word processing. They probably aren't ready for official keyboarding classes in the primary grades, but they can "hunt and peck" little stories, type sentences, or even create simple family newsletters. Children who struggle with handwriting are delighted to write little projects on the computer and print out an attractive story. There is no need to require that they write a rough draft. They can do their draft on the computer, and they learn how to erase and change words quickly and easily. They even become comfortable with checking their spelling.

Depending on your children's interests, middle and high school students can enroll in programming classes, use the Internet for research projects, and participate in computer camps or classes. All of these outlets can provide technological education as well as social fun for gifted kids.

Unfortunately, the exciting learning opportunities provided by the Internet also carry some risks; however, with reasonable precautions, parents can prevent most Internet-related problems. Children who have been brought up using computers find the Internet a delightful opportunity to explore new worlds without leaving their computer keyboard. They may follow their curiosity to discover information on almost any topic. The "almost any topic" is part of the problem because there are so many topics on the Internet that children are not mature enough to learn about. Furthermore, the Internet permits communication with both the child and adult worlds. Children's voices are disguised by the anonymity of the computer, and they cannot be differentiated by other adults using the Internet. The anonymity actually can be socially helpful for shy or fearful children. The overriding concern is that the exposure to so much adult information and communication provides teens with a pseudo-sophistication that permits them to make decisions they haven't the wisdom or experience to make.

Parents often are intimidated by their adolescents who may know more about Internet use than they do. Although parents know they should provide guidance, they're not sure of how much or how to restrict their children's use. Despite technology's efforts to provide assistance to parents, parents often don't know how to use the technology. Computer software stores can provide information on appropriate screening programs, and computer science teachers can also be helpful to parents.

The Internet has created new areas of conflict between parents and children. Although the family challenge of the Internet is in some ways similar to the challenge of too much adolescent telephone talk, the complexities of the Internet multiply the struggles that some parents have with their children. If adolescent-parent relationships are reasonable, Internet issues will be a matter of clear communication and acceptable limits. On the other hand, if relationships are troubled (and many are during the teenage years), the Internet may add to family struggles.

Parents should sit down with their teenagers to negotiate an agreed upon time for Internet use. That Internet time should begin only after homework is complete (unless the Internet is being used to gather homework information). Parents should try to be positive about the teenager's use of the Internet and explain that if they're using it for educational or social purposes, that's a good thing. However, kids must be cautioned not to provide their address or telephone number to *anyone*. There have been a number of publicized experiences in which providing this information has caused major problems for teens. Here are some further guidelines for Internet use:[38]

➤ Always have good manners and be polite when talking to someone else online.

➤ Ask your parents to spend time with you while online so that you can show them some of the neat things you can find online.

➤ Only use the Internet when your parents tell you it's okay, and only for as long as you are supposed to.

➤ Don't give out personal information like your address, telephone number, or school name to anyone unless you have permission from your parents.

➤ Don't break copyright rules by taking words, pictures, or sound from someone else's website without their permission.

➤ Never meet with a cyberfriend or key pal unless your parents go with you or you have their permission to go alone.

➤ Don't respond to any e-mail messages you get if they are strange, mean, or upsetting to you, and tell your parents or teachers right away.

➤ Don't send pictures of yourself or your family to anyone unless you have permission from your parents.

➤ Stop right away if you see or read something on a website that upsets you, and tell your parents or teachers about it.

➤ Don't put words, pictures, or sounds on other people's websites without their permission.

Despite the risks, computers and the Internet continue to provide new and exciting challenges for gifted children.

41
Profoundly Gifted Children

There can be great differences among intellectually gifted children. The term "profoundly gifted" is thus used to designate children who earn an IQ of 145 or above, which in statistical terms is three standard deviations above the mean. When parents read about children with IQ scores of 180 or 190, those are derived from tests that permitted young children to continue to answer items that were very difficult for children their age. Those tests typically did not use national norms but were based on a formula proposed by Alfred Binet that recommended dividing the mental age by the chronologic age and multiplying the result by 100 to arrive at an IQ score. In earlier IQ tests, subtests were arranged by age level, and children would be given three or four months' credit for each subtest completed correctly. The child would continue with tests until he or she had failed a whole age level of subtests. The months of credit were added up to arrive at a child's mental age. There are no current tests that are arranged in that manner.

When gifted children are individually evaluated using IQ or typical achievement tests, it can sometimes be difficult to differentiate children who score in the top 3% of the national norm from those who score in the top one-tenth or one-hundredth of 1%. In Key 8, the author described ceiling scores that limit the identification of extraordinary intellectual ability.

Most IQ tests today have highest scores of only 155 or 160, and to earn those scores, a child must be evenly gifted in all areas. Very few children actually achieve these scores. When the popular Wechsler tests are used and children attain a 19 standard score on any subtest, they have achieved at the ceiling score in that part of the test and the extent of their giftedness isn't really represented in that particular area. If a child scores 19 on two or three of the 10 subtests of the Wecshler tests, the calculated IQ may be an extreme underestimate of the child's actual high ability. A new approach to scoring the WPPSI-III and the WISC-IV can incorporate the earlier used Alfred Binet formula. It provides possibilities for differentiating profoundly gifted children. For example, a child whose IQ was 145 when the WISC-IV was scored in the typical way actually scored 175 when using this age-equivalent score and the classic Binet formula. This paints a very different and more accurate picture of the child's unusual capacity to learn.[39]

There are excellent reasons for differentiating between profoundly gifted children and those who are in the very superior or more typical gifted range of ability. Profoundly gifted children often should have subject and grade skipping in addition to the enrichment given to other gifted children. They tend to be more extremely different in many ways than are the gifted children whose IQ scores measure in the 130s, both in their extensive ability to learn, as well as in the social-emotional differences they may be experiencing.

Although there are school districts that provide special schools and services for profoundly gifted children, there are many more that don't. Parents of such children often have to advocate very patiently to find appropriate programming for these children who may be so accelerated that they are ready for a college education when their chronological peers are in middle school. Although these children may also be socially and emotionally mature beyond their ages, rarely are they totally even in their development, making it considerably more difficult to know how to guide them. Profoundly gifted children may need a combination of schools to provide for their needs. Attending a community college or a high school combined with a university while only age 10 or 12 is one example, but each child is so unique that programs need to be individually planned around both their academic and social–emotional needs.

42

Gifted Schools

Schools that are designed specifically for gifted students are often successful in providing for the variety of needs of such children. These may be specialty elementary or high schools within a public school district or privately run schools.

Urban areas often provide magnet public schools for gifted children. Twelve states now have state-supported residential schools that target mainly science and mathematics. Additional schools are in the process of being created. A list of these is provided among the Resources at the end of the book. These are further discussed in Key 15 related to teenagers.

Sometimes, public schools create a school-within-a-school concept, which can provide individualized curriculum, a gifted peer group, and activities with regular-program students as well. For example, a public elementary school could house four classes of each grade, one of which is designated as a gifted classroom. Children might mix for classes like gym, music, art, and recess but be separate for academic subjects. Some parents would prefer their children mix socially with children of differing abilities in order to appreciate and value the variations among potential friends, while others find the more homogenous class setting of a totally gifted school provides plenty of variety and exposure. Some parents will be concerned about intellectual elitism, while others feel gratified that their children's learning will not be slowed by a classroom with children who are less capable of rapid and in-depth learning.

Not all private schools target the needs of gifted children. Before choosing a private or independent school, parents will want to specifically ask the admissions director about how the school provides for the special needs of gifted children. If the response includes a statement like "All students in this school are gifted," you should be suspicious and investigate further to determine whether that is an accurate description. Sometimes it is correct, because the acceptance standards for admission to the school are very high and the program is actually targeted toward gifted children. Other times, it may only be the school's manner of stating that they will not provide special accommodations for your gifted children. The tone in which that statement is given is likely to reflect either positive or a derisive negative attitude toward gifted children. In addition to questioning the admissions director, parents will want to observe classes, talk to teachers, and notice whether children are all working at similar levels or whether curriculum is truly differentiated for the variety of needs of students. Parents will also want to ask if curriculum acceleration beyond grade level is permitted within the school, since many gifted children thrive in accelerated curriculums.

The National Association for Gifted Children (NAGC) has a specific division devoted to schools for gifted children. Schools included in the Special Schools Division that particularly target the needs of gifted children are included among the Resources at the end of the book.

Important Principles

Principles for Encouraging Learning

1. Enjoy learning experiences with your children.

2. Provide books, resources, and early library opportunities.

3. Answer your children's questions, and give them the opportunity to find answers.

4. Ask your children open-ended questions that may have divergent answers.

5. Encourage and enjoy your children's sense of humor, and help them to laugh at their own mistakes.

6. Provide in-depth home enrichment opportunities.

7. Recognize the fine line that separates support from pressure.

8. Encourage active rather than passive learning.

9. Encourage some time alone in a quiet environment on a daily basis.

10. Identify mentors for your children, and be one for other gifted children.

11. Try to arrange a challenging school environment with your children's teachers.

12. Become directly involved in community support of gifted programs.

Principles for Encouraging Appropriate Family Structure

1. Stay united with your children's other parent(s), if there is another parent, and be willing to make compromises.

2. Give messages of respect for your children's teachers.

3. Be positive about your own career.

4. Encourage children to compete as good sports, but not only in athletics.

5. Be a positive role model of activity, perseverance, and hard work.

6. Don't rescue your children from reality. Stealing their struggles steals self-confidence.

7. Place school effort and learning first, before sports or social life.

8. Keep a separate adult status for you and your adult partner without giving children adult status too soon.

Questions and Answers[40]

My daughter learned the alphabet while listening to a cassette before she was two. We bought her a puzzle with letters, and she had them memorized by the time she was two and a half. Now she is four and reading. She is mature for her age in many ways; I can't go anywhere without someone saying, "I can't believe she's only four."

The problem is that her birthday is June 5, and the kindergarten cut-off date is June 1. The schools are very rigid about this. Our only option seems to be sending her to a private Catholic preschool where they teach the alphabet and how to count to 10 (she can already count infinitely). They promise to keep her busy and out of trouble and will even let her work ahead if she needs to.

You say that children need to be challenged. Are we wasting this gift of hers? Should we push the issue more? Will she have problems in third or fourth grade if she does move into kindergarten?

Your daughter seems to be unusually gifted. If your school district is entirely rigid about early entrance to kindergarten, and some are, you might as well save your energy. If they have any flexibility at all, try to find a professional advocate who will conduct an evaluation of your daughter and obtain some quantitative data, like IQ and achievement test scores, to back up your request. You won't have to worry about your daughter falling behind by third grade unless the school provides no challenge for her. Some children become so bored that they simply stop putting forth any effort.

If your school district won't provide early entrance, find out if there is any small private school in the area that will consider accepting your daughter into their kindergarten on a trial basis. Once she has completed kindergarten, your public school will be obliged to accept her into first grade. Incidentally, if your daughter is truly as capable as you describe, you may have to look for other challenges during her school years. I would also suggest that you get in touch with your state or local gifted children's association for support and information. The National Association for Gifted Children can also be helpful to you; they can be found at www.nagc.org.

I am wondering if I have a gifted child. My son is seven and in the first grade. At age two, he knew all of his colors and shapes and could speak very well. Since the beginning of this past summer, he has been able to read almost anything at third- and fourth-grade levels. He does math on second- and third-grade levels. If he is gifted, how can I enhance his skills even more and keep him interested? He is very inquisitive and eager to learn everything.

Your description of your son sounds as if he is intellectually gifted. Such children often provide special challenges to their parents. You certainly should encourage your son's love of learning. Try to broaden his inquisitiveness and interest in his surroundings so he can enjoy learning about the community, nature, and other people. Encourage his questioning, and enjoy the world of books, music, and movement with him.

Social and emotional learning are also important for your son. While you certainly can be pleased and excited about his learning, it's important that he not learn to define himself only by his brain. Being smart is an advantage, but being a good person extends his ability to make a contribution.

I have an eight-year-old son who has an IQ of 137. We have had him tested and I have asked the school for help, but they refuse. It took them six months to recognize (by advice of their counselor) that he was indeed gifted.

The psychologist who tested my son said to have him skip third grade. The school tells me my son has behavioral problems and will not allow him to skip. I told them that if they gave my son some challenging work, he would not have the time to misbehave. To me, he does seem hyper, but only when he has nothing to challenge his mind. Does this sound like a normal problem with gifted children? Do gifted children act up if they are not getting enough mental stimulation? If he has something challenging to do that he likes, he will work on it until he masters it. If it is something he already knows, he gets bored. He cries not to go to school because he says he is bored there, and he's tired of hearing the teacher explain things "for an hour." The psychologist also said to get him into a Mensa Group, but I can't find one in the area. Can you tell me whom to contact about this?

Although it is true that gifted boys who are unchallenged in school sometimes act up, your son also may be misbehaving for reasons other than boredom. He probably knows about your disagreements with the teacher and assumes that she is wrong; thus, he has the right to be disruptive. You do need to make it clear to your son that there is absolutely no excuse for his behavior, and he may need to learn that the world doesn't revolve entirely around him. Furthermore, a little boredom is simply part of life.

The psychologist who tested your son can help you determine if he is truly unchallenged and may be able to meet with the teacher to make some suggested changes in your son's curriculum so he can learn successfully in school. If there is a gifted coordinator in the school, you could also talk to that person or the principal. A grade skip may be appropriate, and it is possible that his behavior will improve after he is skipped.

Find out about Mensa at www.mensa.org; or to find out about a parent organization for gifted children, contact your state department of education or the National Association for Gifted Children at www.nagc.org.

We have applied to a good private school for our son but are confused about what to do. With four children, we can't afford to send all four to private school and would rather have all our children at the same school. At first, our seven-year-old (oldest) first-grader thrived in public school. Overall, he is a happy child who is easy going, follows instructions, works well independently, and has good friends. But in school, he is not really challenged and says he is bored. He is in a gifted pull-out program two times a week for about an hour each. Our son reads fourth- to sixth-grade material. His class is just beginning to add double digits, which our son could do in kindergarten. He can multiply, do some division, and calculate some fractions. Math used to be his favorite subject, but he hates it now because "it's boring." I am concerned about his attitude. He doesn't want to be different from the other kids. He has expressed a willingness to stay in the present school but understands why we are looking at a private school. I want so badly to know what to do.

Although there are many fine independent schools, there are also many excellent public school systems. Since you cannot afford to send all your children to private school, and you would rather have them all in the same school, why not persevere a bit longer to help the school provide for your son? The psychologist who evaluated your son might suggest grade skipping or some other way for grouping him in special programs within his class. Perhaps you can have his homework replaced by enrichment. There are many options available, and it seems risky to put your family under financial pressure in order for your son to attend an independent school that may or may not provide for his gifted needs. There may be other factors encouraging your son's recent attitude change that also should be investigated. It seems he is beginning a pattern that could lead to underachievement, so you should take his lack of effort seriously.

How do we separate what may be learning disabilities from emotional responses to what goes on in our son's classrooms and school? We have been very frustrated in working with the teachers and counselors, some of whom are well-intentioned but ineffective, and some of whom, sadly, we have discovered, are at least borderline abusive. Whether or not the school can ever correct these teachers' behaviors, we need to help our son gain confidence and tap his talents. He is an outstanding visual artist, very musical, and an excellent creative writer. His weaknesses are in math and social studies, but it is hard to determine how much of that is due to lack of interest. He is known for a sense of humor beyond his years. He is very sensitive, which has made him an easy mark for bullies. We have always encouraged him in his artwork and music.

From the description of your son, it does seem that he is vulnerable to peer and educational issues. First and foremost, I must suggest you get professional help to guide you through the system. Your son's combination of outstanding talent, learning disabilities, and sensitivity all need to be addressed.

Your son's talents can be addressed through private lessons or gifted programming that may be available in your schools. The psychologist can help identify more specifically your son's area of disabilities and advocate for you within the school to help provide an appropriate auxiliary program.

As to your son's sensitivity, the psychologist may also help him to develop social skills that are less likely to make him a victim. He also may need help in safely reporting bullies to the proper authorities.

Most of all, your son needs to continue to have open communication with both of you. You need to listen carefully so you can advocate for him, but you'll also need to be careful that he isn't blaming teachers and other kids in areas where he can assume greater responsibility for himself. Your son's situation is delicate and complicated and requires more assistance than can be given in this short space.

We are parents of two children: one strong-willed, argumentative eight-year-old girl and one easy-going three-and-a-half-year-old boy. Our daughter is prone to extreme temper tantrums and the inability to control her frustration to resolve conflicts. She is gifted and was reading before she entered kindergarten. She has been at the top of her class since kindergarten, but unless she shows more willingness to work on her weaker subjects (such as writing, penmanship, problem solving, getting along with others), her classmates may eventually catch up with her, and that would be a rude awakening.

Though children want to befriend her, she has little tolerance for those whom she feels are less intellectually capable than she. As her first- and second-grade teachers observed, the sarcastic nature of her comments is almost adult-like and far beyond her years.

Thinking that our daughter's problem was that she needed a greater challenge in school, we talked to the principal, and they allowed her to go part-time to a third-grade class while still a second grader. Being with older (and smarter) children seemed to give her some humility.

We are concerned that she may grow up to be smart, talented, and sensitive to her own needs, but can she balance that with love and a conscience with goodwill toward others, and will she be a decent human being? We understand from experts who work with gifted children that much of what's described above is typical of giftedness.

The problems your daughter exhibits are not necessarily related to her giftedness alone, although her unusual ability can trap her into being defensive and competitive. There are many gifted children who do well with other children.

Was your daughter always this difficult, or did she change dramatically after her brother was born? If there was a dramatic change, her behavior might be due to "dethronement," which is described in my book, *How to Parent So Children Will Learn.* Dethronement takes place when a child who received a great deal of attention by adults feels rejected because another child is now receiving much attention. Since your daughter is very verbal, her large vocabulary and adult language may indeed have attracted considerable attention when she was younger. She may be calling out to you, "Notice me; notice me; tell me how smart I am." Now she finds only negative ways to get attention.

Of course, a diagnosis can't be made without knowing your daughter, but she should receive counseling. She should have help with social skills, and you should get help with parenting her. It would be ideal to find a counselor who has special training with gifted children. Although children are born with varying temperaments, there is much that parents can do to prevent small problems from becoming larger ones.

My 16-year-old son was identified as gifted and has started to have a great deal of difficulty in high school. He's supposed to be in eleventh grade but is only in ninth and finds it difficult to continue going to a classroom of kids much younger who make fun of him. I'm very concerned and don't have any idea about what to do. I've always been involved with his school, taken lots of time off work, volunteered at school, and became secretary on the parent council.

I feel somehow that, as the school system always said, "It's the parents' fault that the child doesn't do well in school," or "The child does poorly in school because of what's going on at home." Our home life is pretty quiet and comfortable. Why is it "always the parents' fault?" What else can I do? I'd like my son to graduate from high school at the very least.

Despite the fact that your son was identified as gifted, many things can go wrong both at home and school. Even gifted children can have learning disabilities and emotional problems, and many gifted children underachieve. Usually the problems are a combination of pressures children internalize, as well as school and home environments. Even issues such as peer pressure and sibling competition can cause problems.

While I can't diagnose your son, I suggest you get a professional to get to the root of the problem. If age is becoming a difficult issue, your son might consider studying for a GED, graduating early, and going on to a two-year community college until he is confident enough to transfer to a four-year university. You need to begin by getting help in order to understand what has gone wrong to help your son make fresh attempts at a successful path.

We've been struggling with our 10-year-old son since last year. Third grade was easy, and he was in a gifted program. In fourth grade, he didn't get all the work done quickly and easily, and the gifted program changed its focus from math to a year-long study of architecture. He stopped trying to understand the work and missed assignments. Homework was a battle, and he quit the gifted program one month after school started.

We consulted a psychologist and had our son tested. His IQ is 148, yet he could not care less about school and learning. All he wants to do is watch TV or play video games. We limit his screen time, yet he still manages to avoid doing any extra learning, reading, or projects that interest him because he says they're a waste of time. He fits the profile of an underachiever. My fear is that it's too late. His father is a successful pediatric oncologist who provides quality time to our son and is very involved in the family. I have always modeled good habits about learning; I read a lot, am very involved at school, and am a

coach and den mother for scouts. I don't feel he's overprotected. He received much praise as a child for his intelligence and athletic skills.

Our son wants to go to Harvard and be either a famous actor or a lawyer, but he doesn't want to have to work to achieve those objectives. He continues to see the psychologist, and they're working on perfectionism, lack of confidence, and disinterest in activities he can't have total control over. He has one brother who's a year and a half older and neither gifted nor an underachiever.

Fifth-grade year seems to be going a little better, and he's back in the gifted program. He does just enough to get by and received a D and a C on his first assignments. When extra credit was offered, he didn't do it because he said it wouldn't raise the grade high enough to make the effort worthwhile.

I'm glad your son has been reinstated into the gifted program, because he certainly belongs there, whether he wants to work hard or not. The fact that his older brother works hard and is not considered gifted probably has something to do with your son's problem. He may worry that he will no longer be considered gifted if he works hard. Many gifted children think that the less they have to work at something, the smarter they must be. If they don't get an A after working hard, they fear people will think they're not all that smart.

Another potential possibility related to his brother is that oldest brothers sometimes get the favored place in a relationship with Dad, and the younger brother gets overprotected by Mom. You indicated that you felt you didn't overprotect him, but a good test for you is to determine if you give your younger son the same responsibilities that you did your older son at that age. The competition between brothers close in age all too frequently has the effect of making one an achiever and the other an underachiever.

It's also possible your son has learned to be negative about work by watching his dad work so hard. For example, if you or his dad complain a lot about all the hard work you do, that might cause your son to not want to work. Helping him understand the satisfaction in hard work and letting him know that grades are much less important to you than the fact that he doesn't persevere or carry through and do his best work may make it clearer to him that you value people's efforts.

Consider also that, despite your son's high IQ, it's possible he could have a learning disability or an attention deficit disorder. I assume you may have already discussed these possibilities with your psychologist. If not, you could certainly ask those questions. My book *Why Bright Kids Get Poor Grades* provides many techniques you can apply.

Help! My nine-year-old gifted daughter is very sensitive to general remarks made by teachers in the classroom. For example, "use your best handwriting" can send her into an erasing frenzy. My daughter came home very upset one day because her teacher announced that all permission slips needed to be turned in for an upcoming field trip. She had turned in her permission slip two days prior but was frantic anyway. Even more frightening, while speaking on punishment to a group of third graders, a teacher mentioned youth detention centers and jail for offenders, and my daughter was convinced this applied to her because she was once with a friend who had drawn on the school playground equipment.

Are teachers trained in the harm a broad statement can have on children who are self-motivated to always do and be their best? I've told my daughter many children don't always try as hard as she does and the teacher's comments were meant for them, but she is still troubled.

Your daughter needs help in becoming less sensitive. Teachers' statements like "use your best handwriting" and "all permission slips should be turned in" shouldn't be alarming to a nine-year-old, and it's important not to blame the teacher for your daughter's over-anxiousness. If your daughter's anxiety or perfectionism is causing her to overreact to such basic statements, I would suggest you explain to your daughter that you expect her to always try her best, but that she needn't ever be "the best" at anything. You can also say, "Your teacher's reminder was for the whole class. If you always do your best, that will be fine, but there are some children who require extra reminders."

While it's good for children to be motivated, it's also important for your daughter to understand that no one can be perfect. Perhaps if you or her dad can model how you cope with your own mistakes, it will help her. For example, you could say, "That dinner didn't turn out exactly as I had planned, but I guess it tasted pretty good anyway."

It will also help your daughter if you don't worry too much about her anxiety. Be very matter-of-fact about things that she's finding herself so upset about. Tell her you want to save your worrying for those things that are serious problems, and it will be better if she does too. If your daughter does continue to be very anxious, you'll want to take her to see a psychologist for an evaluation.

I have a student in my fifth-grade class who is tops at playing chess but always calls himself stupid. I asked him why he thought he was stupid, and he said his father said he was. I asked why, and he said because he wasn't fast enough with his multiplication tables. (He scored 99% on the quantitative part of his achievement test.) I explained that this may be a way for his father to encourage him to excel, and he really doesn't mean that he's stupid. We talk quite often, and he tells me how his chess coach is getting him to take risks. I've gotten him to the point that when he enters the classroom and I ask how he is, he says "good" or "great" instead of "bad," as he used to.

This past weekend, a friend of mine saw his father have him against a wall lecturing him during a chess match. I

asked him today how his tournament went, and he said "bad." I commented that sometimes competition is good. He agreed. I was just wondering if you had any suggestions.

It seems by your friend's description that this young man's father may be putting too much pressure on him. If the parents come in for conferences, you might point out to them that their son is very bright and capable but sometimes seems sad and negative. You could then suggest that they consider counseling for him. Whether or not they take him for counseling, they'll at least have heard your concern and may interpret that as a message to back off a little.

Competitive games and tournaments do put pressure on children, but kids can learn to handle them better if they're told that no matter how good they are at something, there'll always be those who are better and, fortunately for them, those who are worse. What's most important is that they do the best they can, learn from their mistakes, and feel good about their improvements. Good sports know that you win some, you lose some, and no one wins all the time. Of course, you can allow them to feel disappointed, but they need to consider how disappointed others are when they win. Those kinds of messages can be very reassuring to your student.

It's also helpful for a competitive child to become involved in some activities that aren't competitive and are just for fun. For example, hiking, biking, or camping can provide releases for his energy and are collaborative with kids doing things together rather than trying to beat each other. If your student learns to enjoy non-competitive activities as well as contests, he'll be able to cope with the pressures of competition better.

My son has a November birthday. He's a very bright kid who does extremely well both at school and in his after-school activities. The teachers recommended that he be placed in first grade last year, but we decided to let him stay in kindergarten and enrich his knowledge outside of

school time. This year, the teacher recommended moving him up to second grade. Again, I have concerns.

By giving my son an extra year, I believe I'm giving him the gift of time. Is it necessary to rush a child early on? I can motivate and cultivate his love of learning by giving him more time to read, watch educational programs, and develop interest in other things. I feel that if he's given more time to relax, play with friends, and pick up skills outside the classroom, it should benefit him for a lifetime! My son does a lot outside of school, including soccer, basketball, and swimming. He goes to Chinese school and Sunday school, participates in chess club, and takes piano lessons.

We're in a very good school district. He's in a first- and second-grade combination class this year. At the beginning of the school year, the teacher told us that all kids in this class will be taught second-grade math, but grades one and two will be separated during reading and writing classes. Since the teacher thinks my son has passed his benchmarks in second-grade reading and writing, she has placed him with the second graders in those subjects. The school is waiting for my consent to classify him as a second grader. We agreed to monitor his progress for another few months before we make a decision.

Any advice will be much appreciated.

It appears that your son is successfully accomplishing second-grade math, reading, and writing, and his teacher believes he should be grade skipped from first grade into second grade. You're hesitant because you believe academic challenge may interfere with his extracurricular and sports activities. You haven't mentioned any concerns about emotional or social adjustment, but perhaps you're also worried about those issues.

Let me reassure you that teachers rarely recommend grade skipping unless they recognize that the child will make a very good overall adjustment. While being young in his grade could interfere with your son's ability to be competitive in basketball, it's unlikely to interfere with soccer, swimming, Chinese, chess, or piano. Because he's only a little younger than some students in his grade, it may not even be obvious to others that he's skipped a grade.

There's a great risk of your son remaining in first grade without the peer academic challenge he should be getting with second graders. He'll believe that you're prioritizing sports above academic achievement, and while I agree that it's good for kids to play sports, the primary purpose of school is to learn academic material. If schoolwork is too easy, your son will soon become bored and turn off school. You wouldn't be pleased if he became an underachiever and refused to do his "too easy" assignments because they were boring. Furthermore, if he underachieves by middle or high school, you won't be happy to hear him say that his grades are low because he thinks that sports and extracurricular activities are more important than school learning. He would be echoing the emphasis you're placing on nonacademic activities, and it could negatively affect his lifelong accomplishments.

There's a large body of research that documents that grade skips for gifted children who are ahead academically are effective for encouraging both academic achievement and better emotional adjustment. While there's no hurry to classify him as a second grader this year since he's in a split grade and grouped with the second graders anyway, it would seem appropriate to move him ahead to third grade next year if the teacher continues to make that recommendation. Furthermore, being in a mixed-grade class is an ideal opportunity to change his grade placement. If you have doubts, I recommend that you request an evaluation by the school psychologist or by a private psychologist who specializes in gifted children to discuss your questions further. It would be important to review your son's IQ and achievement test scores before you make the final decision. His adjustment in working with second graders this year may also convince you.

My 12-year-old daughter is struggling with the fact that she's gifted. She says it makes her a "freak" at school. Other kids call her "the brain," making her feel like she's not a normal kid. She's well liked and gets along with everyone in her grade, but that isn't enough to make her feel good about being smart. What can I do to help her through this?

Middle school can be a difficult time for gifted kids because popularity becomes the most important status goal. Gifted kids often experience very mixed feelings during this time, and they require a tremendous amount of parent support and encouragement to stay on the right track and value their excellent abilities. Actually, in my research for my book *Growing Up Too Fast: The Rimm Report on the Secret World of America's Middle Schoolers*, I found that most middle school kids want to feel above average, but sometimes being identified as a "brain" makes them feel too different and isolated from others. You can help your daughter to feel good about her abilities by assuring her that years from now, she'll be very happy that she's smart, and kids will no longer worry about the popular label. Being smart, creative, and hard working will undoubtedly lead her to friends who share her values and career success. You can also reassure her that there are many other gifted kids who probably feel the ambiguity she's feeling, both in her school and in many other schools. If she gets involved in areas of her skills and interests, she'll undoubtedly find friends who value her skills. Computer clubs, debate, drama, music, math teams, Girl Scouts, science clubs, creativity teams, and art classes are a few of the areas that will help her to find kids who share her talents or interests. You may wish to enroll her in a summer program for gifted students so that she can meet other gifted children who will help her to feel less lonely with her giftedness.

In my *See Jane Win*® research on the childhoods of over 1,000 successful women, many of the women remembered difficult conflicts during the middle and even high school years. They resolved those problems, typically, by finding like-minded kids who shared their love of learning. That should certainly inspire your daughter. She'll actually enjoy my book *See Jane Win® for Girls,* written specifically for girls her age.

I have a seven-year-old daughter who is a major challenge for me. How do you deal with an over-confident child who wants to change the world right now?

I think my daughter is profoundly gifted. I home schooled her until this year, when she requested that I put her in "regular" school like "normal kids," so I did. She's in first grade but could easily be in third or fourth grade. The school just completed an assessment, and I will get the results next month.

She constantly begs me to convert our garage into a science lab so she can do experiments to find a cure for cancer, or to purchase her a warehouse where she would have room to build large robotic machines. She built a robot for the school science fair and won 1st place at her school and 2nd place in the district. She even ran away from home recently—packed her suitcase, and got to the end of the street before I convinced her to come back. She said I didn't understand and appreciate her desire to be a famous scientist today—now, not in the future.

My daughter feels she shouldn't have to go to school or be home schooled, and she should just be left alone to pursue her own ideas and inventions. She's very angry with me for "wasting her time doing baby stuff" at school. She loves her friends and the social aspect of school but feels school is beneath her. Her teacher is a wonderful certified gifted teacher, but my daughter has recently become disrespectful to her because she caught the teacher making a mistake about something. I'm very distressed about this and don't know what to do. Have you seen these types of kids before? What's the best way to handle them, and how do I handle her anger with me?

Even if the school evaluation finds your daughter to be profoundly gifted, she has much more to learn before she's ready to cure cancer. Reading biographies of famous scientists and planning a visit to interview a scientist about the education required for serious scientific research could help her put the depth required for scientific discovery into perspective. While we want to value her wish to make a contribution to society, she'll need to learn to respect those who have the responsibility to teach her much that she doesn't know. It would also be important for her to understand that even smart teachers can make occasional mistakes, but a mistake should be no excuse for her to be disrespectful to her teacher.

Your daughter's problems may, in part, be related to her being gifted and not being provided with challenge in school. First-grade work may indeed seem nonsensical to a child who can read at third- or fourth-grade level. Her problems are also likely to be related to her being overempowered. While I'm not certain of why she believes *she* knows exactly what she needs, I expect that adults in her life have given her too many choices and too much praise and attention for her intelligence. That can happen easily with a uniquely gifted child; it can also happen with home schooling if the parent/teacher gives the child too much power. Your daughter does have the right to be challenged and learn in school, and there are approaches to differentiating her curriculum so that it's appropriate to her skills and abilities. It's important for her to realize that there are adults who may know what's best for her and that she can count on them.

Explain to your daughter that she'll need to be patient until the school and you have set up an educational plan for her. The school may find a grade skip appropriate, but it's unlikely that you'll need to build her a personal laboratory at this time.

Resources

Additional Reading for Parents

Benson, P. L. (2004). *Parenting at the speed of teens.* Minneapolis, MN: Free Spirit.

Benson, P. L., Galbraith, J., & Espeland, P. (1998). *What kids need to succeed: Proven, practical ways to raise good kids.* Minneapolis, MN: Free Spirit.

Beyer, R., Winchester, J. D., & Kent, J. D. (2001). *Speaking of divorce: How to talk with your kids and help them cope.* Minneapolis, MN: Free Spirit.

Bloom, B. S. (Ed.). (1985). *Developing talent in young people.* New York: Ballantine.

California Association for the Gifted. (2003). *Advocacy in action: An advocacy handbook related to gifted and talented students* (2nd ed.). Author.

Clark, R., Hawkins, D., & Vachon, B. (1999). *The school-savvy parent: 365 insider tips to help you help your child.* Minneapolis, MN: Free Spirit.

Davidson, J., Davidson, B., & Vanderkam, L. (2005). *Genius denied: How to stop wasting our brightest young minds.* New York: Simon & Schuster.

Davis, G. A. (1992). *Creativity is forever* (3rd ed.). Dubuque, IA: Kendall/Hunt.

Davis, G. A. & Rimm, S. B. (2004). *Education of the gifted and talented* (5th ed.). Needham Heights, MA: Allyn & Bacon.

Delisle, J. & Galbraith, J. (2002). *When gifted kids don't have all the answers: How to meet their social and emotional needs.* Minneapolis, MN: Free Spirit.

Drew, N. (2000). *Peaceful parents, peaceful kids: Practical ways to create a calm and happy home.* Minneapolis, MN: Free Spirit.

Frankel, F. (1996). *Good friends are hard to find: Help your child find, make, and keep friends.* Minneapolis, MN: Free Spirit.

Galbraith, J. (2000). *You know your child is gifted when....* Minneapolis, MN: Free Spirit.

Goertzel, V., Goertzel, M., Goertzel, T., & Hansen, A. (2003). *Cradles of eminence: Childhoods of more than 700 famous men and women.* Scottsdale, AZ: Great Potential Press.

Greenspon, T. S. (2001). *Freeing our families from perfectionism.* Minneapolis, MN: Free Spirit.

Halsted, J. W. (2002). *Some of my best friends are books: Guiding gifted readers from preschool to high school.* Scottsdale, AZ: Great Potential Press.

Isaacson, K. (2002). *Raisin' brains: Surviving my smart family.* Scottsdale, AZ: Great Potential Press.

Kerr, B. A. (1997). *Smart girls: A new psychology of girls, women, and giftedness.* Scottsdale, AZ: Great Potential Press.

Kerr, B. A. & Cohn, S. J. (2001). *Smart boys: Talent, manhood, and the search for meaning.* Scottsdale, AZ: Great Potential Press.

Matthews, D. J. & Foster, J. F. (2005). *Being smart about gifted children: A guidebook for parents and educators.* Scottsdale, AZ: Great Potential Press.

Piirto, J. (2004). *Understanding creativity.* Scottsdale, AZ: Great Potential Press.

Rimm, S. (1991). A bicycle ride: Why we need grouping. *How to Stop Underachievement Newsletter, 1*(3).

Rimm, S. (1991). Teaching competition to prevent and cure underachievement. *How to Stop Underachievement Newsletter, 2*(2).

Rimm, S. (1992). *Sylvia Rimm on raising kids.* Watertown, WI: Apple.

Rimm, S. (1995). *Why bright kids get poor grades—And what you can do about it.* New York: Crown.

Rimm, S. (1996). *How to parent so children will learn.* New York: Three Rivers.

Rimm, S. (2005). *Growing up too fast: The Rimm Report on the secret world of America's middle schoolers.* Emmaus, PA: Rodale.

Rimm, S., Rimm-Kaufman, S., & Rimm, I. (1999). *See Jane Win®: The Rimm Report on how 1,000 girls became successful women.* New York: Crown.

Rivero, L. (2002). *Creative home schooling: A resource guide for smart families.* Scottsdale, AZ: Great Potential Press.

Rogers, K. B. (2002). *Re-forming gifted education: How parents and teachers can match the program to the child.* Scottsdale, AZ: Great Potential Press.

Ruf, D. (2005). *Losing our minds: Gifted children left behind.* Scottsdale, AZ: Great Potential Press.

Shay Schumm, J. (2005). *How to help your child with homework: The complete guide to encouraging good habits and ending the homework wars.* Minneapolis, MN: Free Spirit.

Smutny, J. F. (2000). *Stand up for your gifted child: How to make the most of kids' strengths at school and at home.* Minneapolis, MN: Free Spirit.

Strip C. A. & Hirsch, G. (2000). *Helping gifted children soar: A practical guide for parents and teachers.* Scottsdale, AZ: Great Potential Press.

Treffinger, D. J., Isaksen, S. G., & Fierstein, R. L. (1982). *Handbook of creative learning.* Williamsville, NY: Center for Creative Learning.

Webb, J. T., Amend, E. R., Webb, N. E., Goerss, J., Beljan, P., & Olenchak, F. R. (2005). *Misdiagnosis and dual diagnoses of gifted children and adults: ADHD, bipolar, OCD, Asperger's, depression, and other disorders.* Scottsdale, AZ: Great Potential Press.

Webb, J. T., Gore, J. L., Karnes, F. A., & McDaniel, A. S. (2004). *Grandparents' guide to gifted children.* Scottsdale, AZ: Great Potential Press.

Webb, J. T., Meckstroth, E. A., & Tolan, S. S. (1982). *Guiding the gifted child.* Scottsdale, AZ: Great Potential Press.

Yahnke Walker, S. (2002). *The survival guide for parents of gifted kids: How to understand, live with, and stick up for your gifted child.* Minneapolis, MN: Free Spirit.

Magazines and Newsletters

Gifted Child Quarterly
Gifted Child Today
Parenting for High Potential
Sylvia Rimm On Raising Kids Newsletter
1. Volume 5, Issue 4, p. 8, 1995
2. Volume 11, Issue 2, pp. 4–5, 2000
3. Volume 12, Issue 4, pp. 3–4, 2002
4. Volume 14, Issue 2, p. 8, 2003
5. Volume 14, Issue 4, p. 8, 2004
6. Volume 16, Issue 3, 2006
Twice-Exceptional Newsletter

Additional Reading for Children

Addherholdt, M. & Goldberg, J. (1999). *Perfectionism: What's bad about being too good.* Minneapolis, MN: Free Spirit.

Fox, A., Kirschner, R., & Verdick, E. (2005). *Too stressed to think?* Minneapolis, MN: Free Spirit.

Galbraith, J. (1999). *The gifted kids' survival guide: For ages 10 & under.* Minneapolis, MN: Free Spirit.

Galbraith, J. & Delisle, J. (1996). *The gifted kids' survival guide: A teen handbook.* Minneapolis, MN: Free Spirit.

Huegel, K. (2003). *GLBTQ (Gay, Lesbian, Bisexual, Transgender, Questioning): The survival guide to queer and questioning teens.* Minneapolis, MN: Free Spirit.

Karnes, F. A. (1996). *Competition: Maximizing your abilities.* Waco, TX: Prufrock Press.

Lewis, B. A. (1995). *The kids' guide to service projects: Over 500 service ideas for young people who want to make a difference.* Minneapolis, MN: Free Spirit.

Lewis, B. A. (1998). *The kid's guide to social action.* Minneapolis, MN: Free Spirit.

Palladino, J. (2004). *Finding the college that's right for you.* Minneapolis, MN: Free Spirit.

Rimm, S. (1990). *Gifted kids have feelings too—And other not-so-fictitious stories for and about teenagers.* Watertown, WI: Apple.

Rimm, S. (2003). *See Jane Win® for girls: A smart girl's guide to success.* Minneapolis, MN: Free Spirit.

Rimm, S. & Rimm-Kaufman, S. (2001). *How Jane won: 55 successful women share how they grew from ordinary girls to extraordinary women.* New York: Crown.

Verdick, E. & Lisovskis, M. (2002). *How to take the grrrr out of anger.* Minneapolis, MN: Free Spirit.

Additional Resources for Parents

Websites about Gifted Children

National Association for Gifted Children (NAGC)
www.nagc.org

Council for Exceptional Children
www.cec.sped.org

The Davidson Institute for Talent Development
www.ditd.org

ERIC DIGESTS (Former ERIC Clearinghouse System)
www.ericdigests.org

Hoagies Gifted Education Page
www.hoagiesgifted.org

Leap Frog
www.leapfrog.com

Mensa International
www.mensa.org

Rivanna Music (CDs for teaching early social skills)
www.rivannamusic.com

Supporting Emotional Needs of the Gifted (SENG)
www.sengifted.org

Sylvia Rimm
www.sylviarimm.com
www.seejanewin.com

Twice-Exceptional Newsletter
www.2enewsletter.com

World Council for Gifted and Talented, Inc.
www.worldgifted.org

Learning Lead's Q-Cards

(by Sylvia Rimm, Ph.D., published by Apple Publishing Co.)

Parent Pointers (available in English and Spanish)

Student Stepping Stones

Teacher Tips

Course

Rimm's Parenting for Achievement: Six-Hour Training Course, Including Gifted Module, by Sylvia Rimm, Ph.D. (1994, Watertown, WI: Apple)

DVDs for Parents and Educators

How to Respond Counterintuitively to Dependent and Dominant Gifted Underachievers
by Sylvia Rimm, Ph.D.

The Pressures Gifted Children Feel and Why They Underachieve
by Sylvia Rimm, Ph.D.

The Psychological Importance of Classroom Challenge for Gifted Children's Achievement
by Sylvia Rimm, Ph.D.

A United Front for Gifted Children's Achievement
by Sylvia Rimm, Ph.D.

Parenting Successful Children
by James T. Webb, Ph.D.

Talent Search Websites

United States

The Belin Elementary Student Talent Search (BESTS)
www.uiowa.edu/~belinctr/talent-search
Grades 4-6
FL, GA, IA, IL, IN, KS, MI, MN, MO, MS, NE, OK, TN, TX, WI
Grade 7-9
All states

Carnegie Mellon Institute for Talented Elementary Students (C-MITES)
www.cmu.edu/cmites
Grade 3
PA

Center for Talent Development (CTD), Northwestern University
www.ctd.northwestern.edu
Grades 4-8
IL, IN, MI, MN, ND, OH, SD, WI

Center for Talented Youth (CTY), Johns Hopkins University
www.jhu.edu/~gifted
Grades 2-8
AK, AZ, CA, CT, DE, HI, MA, MD, ME, NH, NJ, NY, OR, PA, RI, VA, VT, WA, WV, DC

Motivation for Academic Performance (MAP), Duke University
www.tip.duke.edu
Grades 4-5
AL, AR, FL, GA, IA, KS, KY, LA, MO, MS, NC, NE, OK, SC, TN, TX

Rocky Mountain Talent Search, University of Denver
www.du.edu/education/ces/rmts
Grades 5-9
CO, ID, MT, NM, NV, UT, WY

Talent Identification Program (TIP), Duke University
www.tip.duke.edu
Grades 7-9
AL, AR, FL, GA, IA, KS, KY, LA, MO, MS, NC, NE, OK, SC, TN, TX

The Washington Search for Young Scholars (WSYS)
University of Washington
www.depts.washington.edu/cscy/talent
Grade 8
WA

Canada

Centre for Gifted Education at the University of Calgary Talent Search
www.acs.ucalgary.ca/~gifteduc/talent.html
Elementary, expanding soon to junior high

TIP/Canada, OISE/University of Toronto
www.tip-canada.org
SAT I in grade 7 or 8

Commonly Used Tests

Achievement Identification Measure (AIM). Watertown, WI: Apple.

Achievement Identification Measure—Teacher Observation (AIM-TO). Watertown, WI: Apple.

American College Testing Program (ACT). Iowa City, IA: American College Testing Group Inventory.

Baldwin Identification Matrix. Monroe, NY: Trillium.

Creative Talent (GIFT). Watertown, WI: Apple.

Frasier Talent Assessment Profile (F-TAP). Mary Frasier, University of Georgia.

Group Achievement Identification Measure (GAIM). Watertown, WI: Apple.

Group Inventory for Finding Interests (GIFFI). Watertown, WI: Apple.

Henmon-Nelson Tests of Mental Ability. Chicago: Riverside.

Kaufman Assessment Battery for Children (KABC). Circle Pines, MN: AGS.

Naglieri Nonverbal Ability Test (NNAT). San Antonio, TX: Harcourt Educational Measurement.

Otis-Lennon Mental Ability Tests. San Antonio, TX: Psychological Corp.

Preschool and Kindergarten Interest Descriptor (PRIDE). Watertown, WI: Apple.

Scales for Rating Behavioral Characteristics of Superior Students. Joseph Renzulli, University of Connecticut, Storrs, CT.

Scholastic Assessment Test (SAT I). New York: College Board.

Stanford-Binet Intelligence, Fifth Edition (SB-V). Chicago: Riverside.

Torrance Test of Creative Thinking. Bensenville, IL: Scholastic Testing Service.

Universal Nonverbal Intelligence for Children (UNIT). Chicago: Riverside.

Wechsler Adult Intelligence Scale, Third Edition (WAIS-III). San Antonio, TX: Psychological Corp.

Wechsler Intelligence Scale for Children, Fourth Edition (WISC-IV). San Antonio, TX: Psychological Corp.

Wechsler Preschool and Primary Scale for Intelligence, Third Edition (WPPSI-III). San Antonio, TX: Psychological Corp.

Woodcock-Johnson Tests of Cognitive Abilities, Third Edition. Chicago: Riverside.

Gifted Schools

Provided by the members of the Special Schools Division of NAGC

The Academy for Gifted Children
8401 Montgomery Road
Cincinnati, OH 45236
(513) 794-1404
www.giftedacademy.org

The Advanced Academy of Georgia
Honors College
Uiversity of West Georgia
Carrollton, GA 30118
(678) 839-6249

The Advanced Program
Trinity High School
4011 Shelbyville Road
Louisville, KY 40207
(502) 736-2196

The Center for Gifted at National-Louis University
Box 364
Wilmette, IL 60091
www.centerforgifted.org

Center for Talent Development
Northwestern University
617 Dartmouth Place
Evanston, IL 60208
(847) 491-3782
www.ctd.northwestern.edu

Center for Talented Youth
Johns Hopkins University
McAuley Hall
5801 Smith Avenue, Suite 400
Baltimore, MD 21209
ctyinfo@jhu.edu
http://cty.jhu.edu
(410) 735-6277
Fax: (410) 735-6091

Davidson Academy for Profoundly Gifted Students
www.DavidsonAcademy.UNR.edu

EAGLE School of Madison
5454 Gunflint Trail
Madison, WI 53711
(608) 273-0309
www.eagleschool.org

Greater Cleveland Gifted Academy
3200 West 65th Street
Cleveland, OH 44102
(216) 651-5209

Infinity Charter School
51 Banks Street, Suite 1
Penbrook, PA 17103-2067
(717) 238-1880
Fax: (717) 238-1190
infinitygifted@verizon.net

Lee Academy for Gifted Education
8613 Twin Lakes Blvd.
Tampa, FL 33614
(813) 931-3316
leeacademy@aol.com
www.leegifted.com

The Logan School for Creative Learning
1005 Yosemite Street
Denver, CO 80230
(303) 340-2444
www.theloganschool.org

Lorain Academy for Gifted Students
307 7th Street
Lorain, OH 44052
(440) 244-0855

Quest Academy
500 N. Benton Street
Palatine, IL 60067
(847) 202-8035
www.questacademy.org

Rainard School for Gifted Learners
11059 Timberline Road
Houston, TX 77043
(713) 647-7246
Lorraine Bouchard, Ed.D. Founder
lorraine.bouchard@rainard.org
www.rainard.org

The Rhoades School
141 S. Rancho Santa Fe Road
Encinitas, CA 92024
(760) 436-1102
www.rhoadesschool.com

Ricks Center for Gifted Children
2040 S. York Street
Denver, CO 80208
(303) 871-2982
www.du.edu/ricks

Rocky Mountain School for the Gifted and Creative
5490 Spine Road
Boulder, CO 80303
(303) 545-9230
www.rms.org

Saturday and Summer Enrichment
The Curry School of Education
University of Virginia
405 Emmet Street S.
P.O. Box 400264
Charlottesville, VA 22904-4264
(434) 924-3182
Fax: (434) 924-0747

UCI Gifted Students Academies
University of California Irvine
5171 California Avenue, Suite 150
Irvine, CA 92697
(949) 824-8927
giftedstudents@uci.edu
www.cfep.uci.edu/gsa

University School at the University of Tulsa
600 South College Avenue
Tulsa, OK 74104
(918) 631-5060
Fax: (918) 631-5065

University of Utah Youth Academy of Excellence
1901 E. South Campus Drive
Salt Lake City, UT 84112-9359
(801) 581-7226

Village Glen School
13130 Burbank Blvd.
Sherman Oaks, CA 91401
(818) 781-0360
www.thehelpgroup.org

High Schools for Academically Talented Students

Alabama School of Mathematics and Science
Mobile

Governor's School for Science and Mathematics
Huntsville, AL

Illinois Mathematics and Science Academy
Aurora

Indiana Academy for Science, Mathematics, and Humanities
Muncie

Kentucky Academy of Mathematics and Science
Bowling Green

Louisiana School for Math, Science, and the Arts
Natchitoches

Massachusetts Academy of Math and Science
Worcester

Mississippi School for Mathematics and Science
Columbus

Missouri Academy of Science, Mathematics, and Computing
Maryville

North Carolina School of Science and Mathematics
Durham

Oklahoma School of Science and Mathematics
Oklahoma City

Texas Academy of Mathematics and Science
Denton

Stanford University EPGY Online High School
epgy.stanford.edu/ohs

College Board Offices

For information on Advanced Placement courses and the College Level Examinations Program, please contact www.collegeboard.org.

National Office
45 Columbus Avenue
New York, NY 10023-6992

Middle States Regional Office
Two Bala Plaza, Suite 900
Bala Cynwyd, PA 19004-1501
(610) 667-4400

Midwestern Regional Office
6111 N. River Road, Suite 550
Rosemont, IL 60018
(866) 392-4086

New England Regional Office
470 Totten Pond Road
Waltham, MA 02451-1982
(781) 890-9150

Southern Regional Office
3700 Crestwood Parkway, Suite 700
Duluth, GA 30096
(770) 908-9737

Southwestern Regional Office
4330 S. Mopac Expressway, Suite 200
Austin, TX 78735-6735
(512) 891-8400

Western Regional Office
2099 Gateway Place, Suite 480
San Jose, CA 95110-1017
(408) 452-1400

Glossary

Academic acceleration. Moving through curriculum material more quickly by compacting lessons, skipping to a higher level in a subject or grade, entering school early, taking college-level courses in high school, or actually entering college before the typical age.

Academic enrichment. Expansion of the curriculum within a particular grade level by including more in-depth material than would normally be included at that grade level.

Attention deficit disorder (ADD). Difficulty with inattention.

Attention deficit-hyperactivity disorder (ADHD). Difficulty with inattention, high energy, and impulsive behavior.

Ceiling scores. The highest possible scores attainable in a particular test. It is often difficult to differentiate among highly gifted children because their achievements and aptitudes exceed typical approaches to testing. Tests are often not difficult enough to measure their academic achievements.

Developmental delay. Uneven development in which some kinds of maturation happen later than others. Developmental delay assumes that there will be catch-up later in that development.

Grade-equivalent score. The score on a test that is average for children at that particular grade level; for example, 10.8 means that a child has scored on a particular test similarly to average children in the tenth grade, eighth month.

Handwriting disability. Difficulty with handwriting and written expression that is appropriate to the child's intelligence level. It is sometimes referred to as dysgraphia.

Heterogeneous grouping. Children of all ability or achievement levels working together in one group.

Home schooling. Education conducted at home by a family member in lieu of or in addition to attendance at school.

Homogeneous grouping. Children learning together who are in a similar achievement or ability range.

IQ Tests. These tests were originally thought to measure actual intelligence. IQ stands for *intelligence quotient*, which was the relationship of mental age divided by chronological age. The quotient was multiplied by 100 to obtain the IQ score. Thus, a child who was 10 years old and passed tests at the 14-year-old level was said to have an IQ score of 140 ($14/10 \times 100 = 140$). IQ tests are no longer considered to actually measure intelligence, but they predict school achievement fairly well. An IQ score above 130 is considered in the very superior or gifted range. An IQ of 145 and above is usually referred to as the profoundly gifted range.

Math disability. Difficulty with learning math that is appropriate to the child's intelligence level. It is sometimes referred to as dyscalculia.

Multipotentiality. Many high abilities that are quite different from one another. Having such a variety of high talents can confuse young adults as they try to select careers.

Perfectionism. The setting of impossibly high standards paired with feelings of inability to ever accomplish these standards. Perfectionism differs from excellence in that the latter represents a high quality that is possible and provides the person with satisfaction.

Plug lock. A lock that can be purchased to control television or computer games. The plug is taken from the wall and placed into the lock to prevent children from watching television when unsupervised.

Reading disability. Difficulty with reading material that is appropriate to the child's intelligence level. It is sometimes called dyslexia.

School phobia. Fear of attending school.

Endnotes

1 In addition to the information here, you may wish to look at www.seng.org/articles_parenting/Webb_TipsForSelecting TheRightCounselorForYourGiftedChild.html.

2 The report, *A Nation Deceived: How Schools Hold Back America's Brightest Students,* summarizes the research. Funded by the Templeton Foundation, this report can be obtained at http://nationdeceived.org.

3 For more information, visit www.giftedbooks.com/bk0910707308.html.

4 For more information about plug locks, ask your local hardware store, search the Internet, or call (800) 795-7466.

5 For more information about Scotopic Sensitivity, please call (800) 795-7466.

6 Rimm, Rimm-Kaufman, & Rimm (1999).

7 A sample of the *Iowa Acceleration Scale* can be seen at www.giftedbooks.com/IAS%20for%20Website.pdf.

8 For more information about plug locks, ask your local hardware store, search the Internet, or visit www.sylviarimm.com.

9 Additional sample conversations and suggestions can be found in *Re-Forming Gifted Education: How Parents and Teachers Can Match the Program to the Child*, by Karen Rogers.

10 For further information, contact CLEP, P.O. Box 6600, Princeton, NJ 08541-6600, phone (800) 257-9558, or e-mail clep@infor.collegeboard.org.

11 Rimm, Rimm-Kaufman, & Rimm (1999).

12 Rimm (1995), p. 405.

13 Rimm (1995, 1996).

14 "Ogre and dummy" games are further described in *Why Bright Kids Get Poor Grades—And What You Can Do about It*, by Sylvia Rimm.

15 Rimm (1995).

16 Parents may also wish to give the grandparents a copy of the book, *Grandparents' Guide to Gifted Children*, by Webb, Gore, Karnes, and McDaniel.

17 Rimm (1996), pp.4-5.

18 Rimm (1992).

19 Rimm (2006).

20 Sylvia Rimm (2002). *On Raising Kids* newsletter, Volume 12 Issue 4, 3-4.

21 Rimm (1995). Reprinted with permission.

22 Adapted from American Psychiatric Association. (2000). *Diagnostic and statistical manual of mental disorders* (4th ed., text revision). Washington, DC: Author.

23 American Academy of Pediatrics. (2000, May). *Pediatrics.*

24 Rimm (1995).

25 Rimm (2006).

26 Treffinger, Isaksen, & Fierstein (1982).

27 Adapted from Osborn, A. F. (1993). *Applied imagination.* Buffalo, NY: CEF. Reprinted with permission.

28 From Sylvia Rimm's Learning Lead's Q-Cards, *Student Stepping Stones.* Reprinted with permission.

29 Rimm (1995).

30 Rimm (1995). Reprinted with permission.

31 Rimm (2003).

32 Rimm (2003), p. 8.

33 Rimm, Rimm-Kaufman, & Rimm (1999).

34 Rimm (2006).

35 Davis & Rimm (2004).

36 Rimm & Rimm-Kaufman (2001).

37 Rimm (2006).

38 Rimm, S. (2004). *On Raising Kids Newsletter, 14*(4), p. 8.

39 Deborah Ruf elaborates on this approach in her book, *Losing Our Minds: Gifted Children Left Behind*, and also describes developmental milestones of gifted children of various levels.

40 The author is a columnist for Creators Syndicate. These questions and answers are from her syndicated column, *Sylvia Rimm On Raising Kids.*

Index

About the Author

D r. Rimm is a psychologist who specializes in working with gifted children. She directs the Family Achievement Clinic in Cleveland, Ohio, and is a clinical professor at Case Western Reserve University School of Medicine. She has authored more than 20 books and hundreds of articles. Her book, *Why Bright Kids Get Poor Grades—And What You Can Do about It*, has been foundational in serving gifted underachievers. Her research on the childhoods of successful women was described in *See Jane Win®*, which was a *New York Times* Bestseller and was featured on the *Oprah Winfrey* and *Today* shows and in *People* magazine. Her book, *Rescuing the Emotional Lives of Overweight Children*, was a finalist for the Books for a Better Life Award. Dr. Rimm also writes a parenting column syndicated nationally through Creators Syndicate and has served for many years on the Board of Directors of the National Association for Gifted Children.

Says Katie Couric, NBC *Today* show long-time host, "Dr. Rimm is a welcome voice of calm and reason—someone who offers practical advice, with almost immediate results. She's a guardian angel for families who need a little or a lot of guidance." Dr. Sylvia Rimm's nine years as a contributing correspondent to NBC's *Today* show and as a favorite personality on public radio make her a familiar child psychologist to many audiences.

Dr. Rimm lives with her husband in Ohio. They have four children and nine grandchildren, and she considers her own experience as a parent to have contributed to her good common sense advice.